English
for
Tourism
Professionals

Reiko Fujita

JN209057

NATIONAL
GEOGRAPHIC
L E A R N I N G

Australia · Brazil · Mexico · Singapore · United Kingdom · United States

English for Tourism Professionals

Reiko Fujita

© 2019 Cengage Learning K.K.

Text Credit:
p. 15: Topic Reading 1 © Ecotourism Kenya

Photo Credits:
p. 13: © vm/iStock.com; p. 15: © Joel Carillet/iStock.com; p. 16: (t) © tropicalpixsingapore/iStock.com, (b) © coleong/iStock.com; p. 18: © kata716/iStock.com; p. 19: © Alamy (RM)/Pacific Press Service; p. 21: © Onfokus/iStock.com; p. 23: © saiko3/iStock.com; p. 25: © Alamy (RM)/Pacific Press Service; p. 27: © f9photos/iStock.com; p. 29: (t to b) © designalldone/iStock.com, © designalldone/iStock.com, © designalldone/iStock.com, © designalldone/iStock.com, © designalldone/iStock.com, © Sudowoodo/iStock.com; p. 31: © jaraku/iStock.com; p. 33: © IGphotography/iStock.com; p. 36: © Yagi-Studio/iStock.com; p. 37: © BLOOM image/BLOOMimage /Getty Images; p. 39: © stellalevi/iStock.com; p. 41: (t) © scyther5/iStock.com, (b) © glegorly/iStock.com; p. 42: © andresr/iStock.com; p. 43: © Alamy (RM)/Pacific Press Service; p. 45: © LKeskinen/iStock.com; p. 49: © Ridofranz/iStock.com; p. 51: © tupungato/iStock.com; p. 54: © Weedezign/iStock.com; p. 55: (t) © olmozott98/iStock.com, (b) © drbimages/iStock.com; p. 57: © DaLiu/iStock.com; p. 61: © Kyodo News/Kyodo News/Getty Images; p. 63: © baranozdemir/iStock.com; p. 65: © JakeOlimb/iStock.com; p. 66: © Ziviani/iStock.com; p. 67: (t) © alexsl/iStock.com, (b, l to r) © anouchka/iStock.com, © gchutka/iStock.com, © Digital Vision/iStock.com; p. 69: © The Asahi Shimbun/The Asahi Shimbun/Getty Images; p. 73: © Papado/amana images/Getty Images; p. 75: © Chris Ryan/iStock.com; p. 77: (t) © pcross/iStock.com, (b) © yesfoto/iStock.com; p. 78: © MyLoupe/Universal Images Group/Getty Images; p. 79: © AID/a.collectionRF/amana images/Getty Images; p. 81: (l) © GCShutter/iStock.com, (r) © oscity/iStock.com; p. 84: © lucky-photographer/iStock.com; p. 85: (t) © Yosuke Tanaka/Aflo/Score by Aflo/Getty Images, (b, l to r) © Massimo Merlini/iStock.com, © Michael Blann/iStock.com, © 1001nights/iStock.com, © Bojan89/iStock.com, © monkeybusinessimages/iStock.com, © avid_creative/iStock.com; p. 87: © PeopleImages/iStock.com; p. 90: © lukyeee1976/iStock.com; p. 91: ©DAJ/amana images/Getty Images; p. 93: © kumikomini/E+/Getty Images; p. 97: © Maskot/Maskot/Getty Images; p. 99: (t) © shironosov/iStock.com, (b, l) © Berkut_34/iStock.com, (b, r) © Spiderstock/iStock.com

For permission to use material from this textbook or product, e-mail to **eltjapan@cengage.com**

ISBN: 978-4-86312-356-4

National Geographic Learning | Cengage Learning K.K.
No. 2 Funato Building 5th Floor
1-11-11 Kudankita, Chiyoda-ku
Tokyo 102-0073
Japan

Tel: 03-3511-4392
Fax: 03-3511-4391

はしがき

　21世紀は観光産業が世界経済を牽引する時代と言われており、観光を目的に移動する人々の数は世界中で毎年劇的に増加しています。国連世界観光機構 (UNWTO) によれば、2017年には世界の観光人口は13億を数え、さらに2030年には18億に達するであろうということです。これだけの膨大な数の人間が観光を目的に地球上を移動することにより、世界に与える影響は計り知れません。2018年現在、世界の観光業界ではSDGs（持続可能な開発目標）がキーワードとして大きく浮上しています。環境・紛争・貧困などの様々な問題が地球を取り巻いていますが、世界に大きな影響を与える力のある観光だからこそ、その目標達成に果たす役割は重要です。一歩間違えば悪い影響を与えてしまう可能性もありますが、一方で、国境を越えた交流、協力、相互理解を促進し、世界の公平な開発や安定、平和に貢献する大きな可能性もあります。観光業で将来活躍したいと思っている皆さんには、より良い観光の在り方を考え実行していっていただきたいと思います。そのためには、世界の観光の舞台でコミュニケーションをとれる力が必要となるでしょう。

　このテキストは、ツーリズムやホスピタリティビジネスなどに興味を持っている日本人学生の皆さんが、明確な目的を持って英語を学べるように書かれています。観光業の主要な場面を抽出し、その場面でのやりとりを扱い、学習者の皆さんがツーリズムのプロとして必要な英語コミュニケーションを楽しみながら学べるよう工夫してあります。将来、皆さんが観光業のコミュニケーターとして自信を持って活躍し、観光業を通して地球市民としての責務を果たすために、このテキストが少しでも役に立てば嬉しく思います。

　最後になりましたが、本書の制作にあたり、惜しみない協力をしてくださったナショナルジオグラフィック ラーニングの吉田剛様をはじめ、デザイン・編集担当の皆様に心より御礼を申し上げます。

藤田玲子

本書の構成と学び方

本書は15のユニットで構成されていて、ツーリズムの主要分野である「旅行業」「航空業」「ホテル業」の3つの柱で成り立っています。目次ページ（Contents）のアイコン、あるいは各ページの右端に示されたアイコンを参照していただければ、必要な分野を選んで学習することができます。

英語を一般英語（General English）として学ぶのではなく、特別な目的のための英語（English for a Specific Purpose）として学ぶことで、学習効果がいっそう高まることが期待できます。「英語を学ぶ」というよりは、「英語で"観光を"学ぶ」という意識を持って取り組みましょう。

■ユニット構成

各ユニットでは、リスニング、スピーキング、リーディングの各スキルに加え、観光産業の基本的な知識を学び、この業界で求められる英語の総合力を養うことのできる構成になっています。ユニット内のアクティビティの概要は以下のとおりです。

Warm-up

専門分野に関する予備知識や関連知識を英語で学習します。

Listening

ダイアログを聞いて、設問に答えます。音声を何度も聞くようにしましょう。

Dialogue Study

ダイアログの内容を読んで確認し、基本的な専門用語や表現を学びます。

Pair Speaking Practice

ダイアログに出てくる重要表現を使った会話練習をします。さらに、Role Playでダイアログのおさらいをします。

Topic Reading

観光業に関連するさまざまな種類の読み物を2点ずつ用意しています。それぞれに設問が付いています。授業の中で、または自宅学習用として適宜利用してください。

Traveling Further

学習したトピックをさらに深く学びたい場合や、時間に余裕がある場合に行える発展学習のヒントです。ライティング練習として、学期中・学期末のプロジェクトやプレゼンテーションのテーマとして、あるいは宿題として適宜お使いください。

Appendices

巻末には、接客表現集、航空会社名や空港名のコード（略式表記）、本文の中に掲載しきれなかった使用頻度の高い専門用語のリスト、本文に出てきた重要語句とその訳を一覧にしたインデックスなどを収録しています。必要に応じて活用してください。

Contents

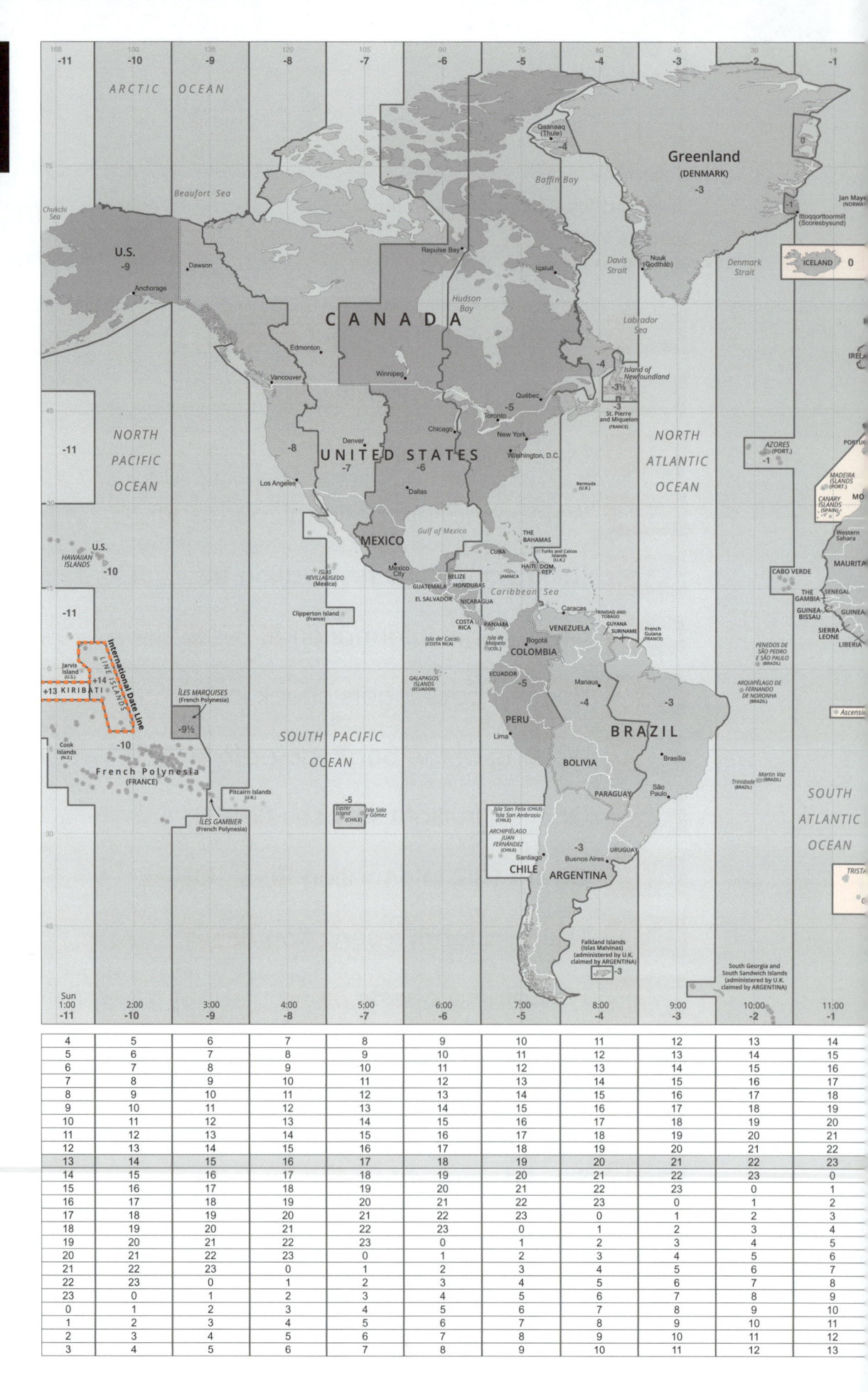

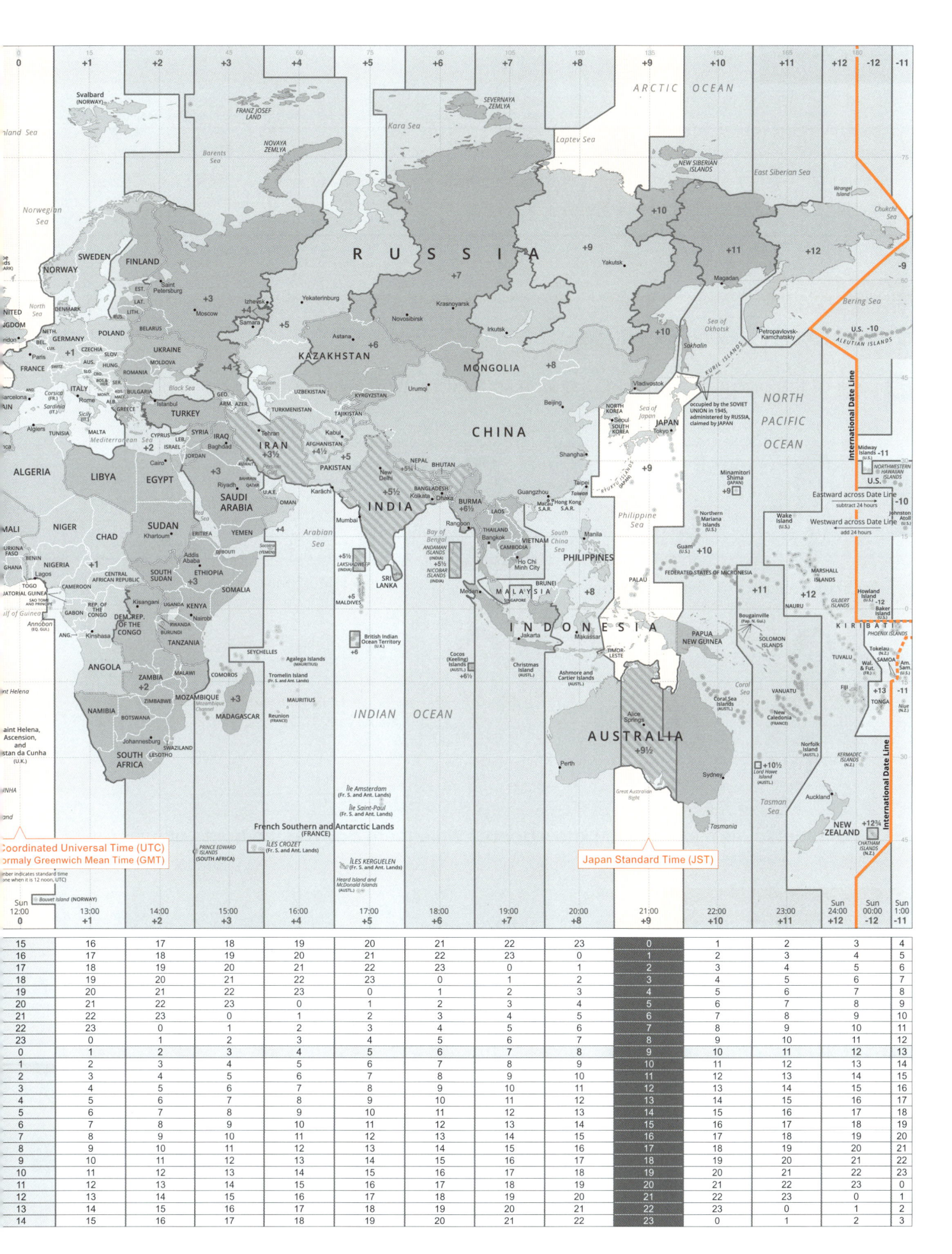

Coordinated Universal Time (UTC)
formally Greenwich Mean Time (GMT)
number indicates standard time
zone when it is 12 noon, UTC)

Japan Standard Time (JST)

Sun 12:00	13:00	14:00	15:00	16:00	17:00	18:00	19:00	20:00	21:00	22:00	23:00	Sun 24:00	Sun 00:00	Sun 1:00
0	+1	+2	+3	+4	+5	+6	+7	+8	+9	+10	+11	+12	-12	-11
15	16	17	18	19	20	21	22	23	0	1	2	3	4
16	17	18	19	20	21	22	23	0	1	2	3	4	5
17	18	19	20	21	22	23	0	1	2	3	4	5	6
18	19	20	21	22	23	0	1	2	3	4	5	6	7
19	20	21	22	23	0	1	2	3	4	5	6	7	8
20	21	22	23	0	1	2	3	4	5	6	7	8	9
21	22	23	0	1	2	3	4	5	6	7	8	9	10
22	23	0	1	2	3	4	5	6	7	8	9	10	11
23	0	1	2	3	4	5	6	7	8	9	10	11	12
0	1	2	3	4	5	6	7	8	9	10	11	12	13
1	2	3	4	5	6	7	8	9	10	11	12	13	14
2	3	4	5	6	7	8	9	10	11	12	13	14	15
3	4	5	6	7	8	9	10	11	12	13	14	15	16
4	5	6	7	8	9	10	11	12	13	14	15	16	17
5	6	7	8	9	10	11	12	13	14	15	16	17	18
6	7	8	9	10	11	12	13	14	15	16	17	18	19
7	8	9	10	11	12	13	14	15	16	17	18	19	20
8	9	10	11	12	13	14	15	16	17	18	19	20	21
9	10	11	12	13	14	15	16	17	18	19	20	21	22
10	11	12	13	14	15	16	17	18	19	20	21	22	23
11	12	13	14	15	16	17	18	19	20	21	22	23	0
12	13	14	15	16	17	18	19	20	21	22	23	0	1
13	14	15	16	17	18	19	20	21	22	23	0	1	2
14	15	16	17	18	19	20	21	22	23	0	1	2	3

Introduction

tourism とは、旅（travel、transportation）・宿泊設備（accommodations）・飲食（restaurants）・観光（entertainment、attractions）などを提供するビジネスのことをいいます。またこの産業分野を hospitality industry とも呼びます。ユニットの学習に入る前に、この業界についての理解を深めておきましょう。

Tourism Jobs

以下の問題に答えて、tourismの仕事を分類してみましょう。

Q1 Look at the pictures of people who work in tourism. Write each job in a box below.

front desk clerk   flight attendant   bellboy

tour guide   airport ground crew   travel agent

Tourism (Hospitality Industry)

■ Travel jobs

■ Hotel jobs

■ Transportation jobs (airlines/trains)

Q2 What other tourism jobs do you know about? Write them down in the boxes above.

Discussion about Travel

3〜4人のグループを作って、以下の質問について話し合ってみましょう。

Q1 Purposes of travel

Why do people take trips? Why do they want to visit other parts of the country or the world? List as many reasons as possible.

Q2 Experiences during travel

If we have a lot of great experiences during our trip, we feel the trip was great. On the contrary, if we experience trouble or things which do not satisfy our expectations, we feel disappointed. Below is the typical progress of a trip. How can tourism workers help the traveler to have a great trip? Write ideas in the box with your group.

🏠 home ➡ airport ➡ arrival ➡ sightseeing ➡ eating ➡ hotel ➡ meeting local people ➡ shopping ➡ nighttime entertainment ➡ return flight ➡ home 🏠

旅行者（tourist）の抱く様々な目的の実現を手助けをするのが、tourismの仕事です。tourismは、旅行者がある場所から出発して帰るまでのあらゆる過程で、満足のいく快適な経験ができるように"travel"という形のない商品を演出します。旅の過程には旅の計画を立てるのを手伝う人、見送る人、世話をする人、案内をする人など、様々な人が関わりを持ちます。この過程にホスピタリティの気持ちを持って関わることで、旅人の経験をより豊かなものにすることができるのです。tourismがhospitality industryと呼ばれるゆえんです。

Tourism and Language

tourismに従事する人はtouristsとのコミュニケーションが欠かせません。どんなコミュニケーション力が必要で、どんな特徴があるでしょうか。以下のまとめを理解した上でUnit 1に進みましょう。

1 Intercultural communication ▶異文化コミュニケーション力

- 様々な文化的背景を持った人々とやり取りすることがあります。その価値観も使用する言語も一様ではありません。文化の違いを乗り越える知識と受容力が求められます。

2 Verbal communication ▶言語コミュニケーション力

- 挨拶がコミュニケーションの基本です。先手必勝で行いましょう。
- お客様を大切にしているという温かい気持ちを言葉にのせましょう。丁寧な言葉とカジュアルな言葉を、その場に応じて使い分けましょう。
- 英語を共通語として使用する場合は、相手が英語を母語としない場合もあります。多様な英語（World Englishes）や片言英語にも対応できるようにしましょう。場合によってはゆっくりと、はっきりと伝えましょう。
- tourism の中で使用頻度の高い専門用語は覚えておきましょう（巻末のインデックスを参照）。

3 Non-verbal communication ▶非言語コミュニケーション力

- 言葉が完全に通じなくても、笑顔やアイコンタクトで相手に気持ちを伝えましょう。
- 言葉が通じにくい場合は、指で示したり、ジェスチャーを使ったりするなどして、相手の理解を促しましょう。

音声ファイルの利用方法

 00 のアイコンがある箇所の音声ファイルにアクセスできます。

https://ngljapan.com/eftp-audio/

❶ 上記URLにアクセス、またはQRコードをスマートフォンなどのリーダー
でスキャン
❷ 表示されるファイル名をクリックして音声ファイルをダウンロードまた
は再生

Recommending a tour

旅行代理店では様々な旅行商品の販売、宿泊や交通機関の予約代行などの業務を行っています。外国人居住者が多い地区では英語での応対も必要です。このユニットでは旅行の情報を求めに来た外国人のお客様への応対を練習しましょう。

Warm-up　3〜4人のグループで、世界の国々について以下の質問に答えましょう。

Q1 Which countries in the world are the most popular tourist destinations? List three countries you think are most popular. Then check your answers with your teacher.

Your group's answer	1.	2.	3.
Answer	1.	2.	3.

Q2 Do you know anything about these tourist destinations? Write down the capitals and main sightseeing spots for each country.

Capital	1.	2.	3.
Sightseeing spot	1.	2.	3.

Listening　旅行代理店での店員（女性）とお客様（男性）のダイアログを聞いてみましょう。 02

A Listen to the audio and check True or False.

1. The customer is interested in going abroad. ☐ True ☐ False
2. The customer is planning to travel with his family. ☐ True ☐ False
3. The price of the tour depends on the airline used. ☐ True ☐ False

B Listen again and answer the following questions.

1. When is the customer planning to take a trip?

2. Which two places does the customer seem to be interested in?

3. What does the customer decide to do?

Travel　Airline　Hotel

[At a **travel agency** in Tokyo]

Travel agent: **Good morning. May I help you?**

Customer: Yes. My family is planning to go on a skiing trip during the Christmas holiday. Can I get some information?

Travel agent: **Certainly.** Are you planning to go abroad or stay in Japan?

Customer: Well, I hear the skiing in Hokkaido is very good, so we are interested in going there.

Travel agent: Great. Here are some **brochures** in English. Niseko and Tomamu are fabulous ski resorts.

Customer: OK. Which one is closer to Sapporo?

Travel agent: Niseko. It is about three hours by train from Sapporo. Here is a map. **Tomamu is located in the mid-western region of Hokkaido.**

Customer: I see. Do you have any **package tours** that include a stay in Sapporo? We are interested in exploring the area **for a day or two**.

Travel agent: In that case, how about this tour? **Four nights** at Niseko resort and two nights in Sapporo.

Customer: That sounds great. So, how much is this tour **per person**?

Travel agent: It depends on when you are going.

Customer: We'd like to leave on Christmas day.

Travel agent: It also depends on which hotel you choose. Here is a choice of hotels—there are **luxury, standard, and economy**. The prices are listed beside the hotel names.

Customer: All right. I will take these brochures home and talk to my family. Thank you for your help.

Travel agent: You're welcome. I hope to see you soon.

Vocabulary and Useful Expressions

travel agency	「旅行代理店」= travel agent, travel bureau
travel agent	「旅行代理店の係員」 代理店そのものも travel agent ということがありますが、係員のことを agent と呼びます。
Good morning. May I help you?	「おはようございます。ご用件をお伺いしましょうか」 接客にあたる際の最初のフレーズです。May I help you? の前に Hello. や Good evening. などの挨拶を入れましょう。How can I help you? も同様に使われます。
customer	「顧客」
Certainly.	「もちろんです」 相手に対し丁寧に応対するときに使います。
brochure	「パンフレット」= pamphlet
Tomamu is located in the mid-western region of Hokkaido.	「トマムは北海道の中西部に位置しています」 〈A is located...B（A は B の…にあります）〉「...」には、near、in the middle [center / north / south / east / west] of などを入れて場所を説明することができます。文型で覚えておきましょう。
package tour	「パック旅行」= package holiday transportation（輸送）や accommodations（宿泊）などがすべて組み込まれた旅行商品。
for a day or two	「1日または2日間」= for one or two days
four nights	「4泊」 「…泊」を night で表現します。
per person	「1人につき」
luxury, standard, and economy	「デラックス、スタンダード、エコノミー」 サービスや施設などにより分類されますが、それぞれの料金に差があります。

Travel
Airline
Hotel

Column

サステーナブル・ツーリズム（持続可能な観光）とは

20世紀に多くの人が気軽に団体で世界中へ旅に出かけるようになったマス・ツーリズム（mass tourism）によって、観光地の自然や遺跡に様々な悪影響がありました。その反省から、21世紀はサステーナブル・ツーリズム（sustainable tourism）が大変重要なコンセプトとなっています。観光地の自然環境を守り、かつその土地の人々の生活向上に貢献できる旅を責任を持ってつくるまたは行う、というのがその思想です。

Pair Speaking Practice

A 旅行代理店の係員とお客様の会話です。下線文を入れ替えて練習しましょう。

03

Travel agent: ¹Good morning. **May I help you?**

Customer: Yes. Can I ²make a reservation?

Travel agent: **Certainly.**

	1	2
1st Time	(at 10 a.m.)	get information on city tours
2nd Time	(at 6:30 p.m.)	buy Shinkansen tickets here
3rd Time	(at 2 :30 p.m.)	have some brochures on tours to China

B お客様に場所を教えましょう。

04

Customer: Where is ¹Tomamu?

Travel agent: It is located ²in the mid-western region of Hokkaido.

	1	2
1st Time	Tokyo Tower	in the center of Tokyo
2nd Time	Hakata	in the north of Kyushu
3rd Time	*think of your own*	*think of your own*

Role Play お客様にツアーの案内をしましょう。
必要なセリフをダイアログから抜き出して覚え、交替でロールプレイをしてみましょう。

Student A	Student B
You are a customer. You want to take a trip to Hawaii during your summer vacation. This is your first visit to Hawaii, so you want to go to Honolulu. Go to a travel agency and get some information.	You are a travel agent. Your customer wants to get some information for a trip to Hawaii. Give your customer a brochure and the information he/she needs.

Enjoy paradise with our low-price package tour!!

Oahu Island 4 days
Enjoy the lively atmosphere of Honolulu and famous Waikiki Beach!
Beach Hotel (standard) ¥250,000 / Season Hotel (luxury) ¥300,000

Hawaii Island 4 days
A quiet vacation in spectacular scenery!
Excel Hotel (luxury) ¥300,000

Oahu and Hawaii Islands 6 days
Enjoy the lively atmosphere of Honolulu, then relax in the natural beauty of Hawaii Island.
Season Hotel in Oahu, Excel Hotel in Hawaii ¥450,000

Topic Reading **1** ケニアの民間団体 "Ecotourism Kenya" の旅行者へのお願いを読んで、質問に答えましょう。

Karibu! Welcome to Kenya, the home of the great African safari!

Our country is blessed with some of the world's richest wilderness areas. In order to preserve this vital biodiversity, we urge all visitors to read the following guidelines and help us protect our natural heritage.

When visiting our country:

1 Travel with qualified safari guides
Traveling with a qualified guide will ensure that you see the very best that Kenya has to offer—without diminishing the experience for future visitors.

2 Support eco-friendly accommodation facilities
A growing number of Kenyan lodges and safari camps are changing to environmentally responsible services, using solar and wind power, keeping rubbish out of protected areas, treating wastewater, and supporting local conservation projects. Please support local conservation work in the areas you visit.

3 Respect local cultures and promote community benefits
Local communities are the custodians of the wilderness of the future. Try to support projects that benefit local people through employment, community development, and the preservation of traditional livelihoods. When you visit local villages, please respect social and cultural customs and ask your guide about appropriate forms of behavior. Always ask permission if you wish to photograph a person, their home or their livestock.

| Vocabulary Notes | ▪ Karibu 「(スワヒリ語で) ようこそ〔英語の welcome に相当〕」 ▪ biodiversity 「生態系の多様性」 ▪ rubbish 「ごみ」 ▪ custodian 「守衛」 ▪ livelihood 「暮らし」 ▪ livestock 「家畜」 |

Travel

Airline

Hotel

Q1 What is the organization asking visitors to choose?

   a. Guides with qualifications

   b. Volunteer guides

   c. Famous guides

Q2 How can you show respect for local cultures?

   a. By taking photographs without asking

   b. By behaving according to your own values

   c. By acting according to your guide's advice

Q3 From this web page, what can we understand "Ecotourism Kenya" wants to do?

   a. Develop many resort facilities to increase the number of tourists

   b. Promote tourism that protects nature and benefits the local people

   c. Keep tourists at minimum to preserve biodiversity

\ Otaru Snow Light Path /   Day Trip from NISEKO

Guided Tour (reservation required)

Price:　　　Adult: 7,000 yen / Child: (up to 11 yrs): 3,500 yen
Dates:　　　February 10–18
Duration:　 7 hours
Schedule:　Daily tour departs from
　　　　　　　Niseko Hirafu Ski Area at 3:00 p.m.
Minimum booking:　1 person

Includes:
- Dinner at a Japanese restaurant: Enjoy a buffet service featuring a variety of Japanese cuisine.
- Mt. Tengu Aerial Cableway: Enjoy the night view of Otaru.
- Otaru Snow Light Path Festival: Stroll along the snow light path near the canal at leisure.

Vocabulary Notes	■ depart「出発する」　■ minimum booking「最少催行人数」　■ buffet「バイキング形式の料理」 ■ cuisine「料理」　■ aerial cableway「ロープウエー」　■ canal「運河」　■ at leisure「自由に」

Q1 What time are we leaving Niseko? And what time are we coming back?

_____

Q2 Do I have to make a reservation for this tour?

_____

Q3 What will we do in Otaru?

_____

Q4 I am taking my wife and a seven-year-old daughter. How much do I need to pay?

_____

Traveling Further

Choose one popular tourist destination country and do research about it. Find out about the capital, main attractions, typical food, geography, climate, etc. Share your findings in class.

Taking a tour booking

旅行申し込みを受ける場合には、お客様の情報を入手したり、支払いの手続きをしたり、正確に作業をこなさなくてはなりません。ここではツアーの予約を受ける練習をしましょう。

Warm-up   3～4人のグループで、世界の国々について以下の質問に答えましょう。

Q1 When you travel abroad next time, do you want to take a package tour or plan and travel by yourself? Why? Why not?

_____

_____

_____

Q2 Discuss the advantages and disadvantages of package tours.

Advantages	
Disadvantages	

Listening   旅行代理店での店員（男性）とお客様（女性）のダイアログを聞いてみましょう。   🎧 05

A Listen to the audio and check True or False.

1. The customer will travel for four days. ☐ True ☐ False
2. The customer is traveling with six family members. ☐ True ☐ False
3. The customer will be receiving documents by mail. ☐ True ☐ False

B Listen again and answer the following questions.

1. On what date does the customer plan to leave on this trip?

_____

2. How much is the tour in total?

_____

3. If the customer needs to cancel the trip, where can she find information?

_____

Travel · Airline · Hotel

[At a travel agency in Osaka]

Travel agent: Good afternoon. How can I help you?

Customer: Hi. We'd like to take your "Bali and **Borobudur** 6 days" tour.

Travel agent: Excellent choice, ma'am. Borobudur is magnificent. You will enjoy it.

Customer: Yes, I hope so. I am very interested in Indonesian history and culture.

Travel agent: Great. When **would you like to** leave**?**

Customer: August 5.

Travel agent: August 5. How many people are there in your **party**?

Customer: Three. Me, my husband, and our six-year-old son.

Travel agent: OK, then your son can travel with the **child fare**. Now, let me just make sure we still have space… *(Checking the computer)* Yes, no problem. Would you like to **book** the tour now?

Customer: Yes, please.

Travel agent: All right. Would you **fill out this form**, please? I need all your names, and your address and contact number.

Customer: Sure… Here you are.

Travel agent: **Mrs. Bates**, **your total** for the whole family **comes to** 270,000 yen. Would you like to pay now?

Customer: Yes. Here is my card.

Travel agent: Thank you. You can find our **cancellation policy** on the back of the brochure. Here is your **itinerary** and receipt. We'll send you a travel **voucher** and the detailed information about two weeks before your trip.

Customer: Great! Thank you.

Vocabulary and Useful Expressions

Borobudur	「ボロブドゥール」 インドネシアのジャワ島にある8〜9世紀の大乗仏教の遺跡。世界遺産に登録されています。
would you like to...?	「…なさりたいですか」 do you want to...? の丁寧な言い方。お客様には do you want to でなく would you like to を使いましょう。 Do you want to book the tour? ⇒ Would you like to book the tour?
party	「ご一行様」 「一団」という意味があります。
child fare	「子供料金」 fare は「運賃」という意味で、adult fare（大人料金）、full fare（正規料金）のように、乗り物を含む旅行代金に使われます。ツアーには price も使われます。 e.g. The prices of package tours go up in summer.
book	「予約をする」= reserve, make a reservation
fill out this form	「この書類に記入する」 fill out は「記入する」、form は「書式」という意味です。
Mrs. Bates	「ベイツ様」 名前がわかった時点からなるべくお客様の名前を呼ぶことで、お客様を大切にしている印象を与えることができます。
your total comes to...	「合計は…となります」
cancellation policy	「取り消し条件、キャンセル規約」 旅行の内容によって違ってきますが、ツアーを申し込んだ場合に渡される旅行条件書に規定が書いてあります。
itinerary	「旅程表」
voucher	「旅行券、宿泊券」 旅費を前払いしているので、旅行中はこの券で支払いをします。

Travel

Airline

Hotel

Column

ツーリズムは21世紀の牽引産業

世界的に国際旅行は増加しており、ツーリズムは巨大産業として成長を続けています。特に近年は新しいデスティネーションが開発され、雇用と事業の創出、輸出収入、インフラ開発を通じて社会経済の発展に重要な役割を果たしてきています。国連世界観光機関（UNWTO）の長期予測によると、世界全体の国際観光客到着数は2030年には18億に達するとされており、観光はまさしく21世紀の繁栄を牽引する産業であるといえるのです。このような中で、旅行業は旅行者と航空会社や宿泊施設をつないだり、旅の企画や提案をしたりと、多岐にわたる業務を担っています。

Pair Speaking Practice

A would like to...を使って丁寧に質問する練習をしましょう。

> Travel agent: Would you like to [1]pay today?
> Customer: Yes, I want to [2]pay today.

	1	2
1st Time	use our telephone	use your telephone
2nd Time	get more information	get more information

B 合計金額を伝える練習をしましょう。

> Travel agent: **Your total comes to** [1]15,000 yen. Would you like to pay now?
> Customer: [2]Yes, here is my credit card.

	1	2
1st Time	19,500 yen	Yes, here is 20,000 yen.
2nd Time	2,980 dollars	Yes, I'd like to pay by credit card.
3rd Time	368,000 yen	No, I will pay later.

Role Play ツアーの予約を受けましょう。
必要なセリフをダイアログから抜き出して覚え、交替でロールプレイをしてみましょう。

Student A	Student B
You are a customer. You came to book the tour "New Zealand 6 days." You plan to leave on July 29 and come back on August 3. You are traveling with two friends. Ask for the total price, but say you will pay at the bank later.	You are a travel agent. Your customer wants to book a tour to New Zealand. Ask for necessary information (date, number of travelers, etc.) and tell the customer the total price—450,000 yen.

Tour Booking Form

Name & contact number	Name	Age	Tel:
Tour name	New Zealand 6 Days		
Tour dates	—		
Other members of your party	Name	Age	
	Name	Age	

Topic Reading 1 — ツアーの日程表を読んで、質問に答えましょう。

Peru—Machu Picchu

Enjoy a visit to Machu Picchu, the "Lost City of the Incas."

7 days—The tour departs from Lima / ends in Lima
$1,095*—price per person, twin share (child up to 11: $650)
Locally hosted *Your international flights are not included.

ITINERARY	
Day 1	Arrive at Lima, Peru (transfer to your hotel)
Day 2	Lima (morning bus tour in Lima, afternoon free)
Day 3	Lima ▼ Cuzco (flight to Cuzco, afternoon free)
Day 4	Cuzco (half-day bus tour in the city, afternoon free)
Day 5	Cuzco ▼ Urubamba (travel to Urubamba)
Day 6	Urubamba ▼ Machu Picchu Ruins (train trip to Machu Picchu) ▼ Cuzco
Day 7	Cuzco ▼ Lima (flight back to Lima)—depart from Lima

Your Travel Value Includes:

- Round-trip travel between the airport and the hotel
- Baggage handling at the airport
- Six breakfasts and four lunches
- Accommodation in first-class hotels (twin-bed rooms)
- All admission charges
- Services of an English-speaking local guide
- Hotel taxes and service charges

Vocabulary Notes
- Machu Picchu「マチュピチュ〔インカ時代の謎の空中都市。世界遺産〕」　■ Lima「リマ〔ペルーの首都〕」
- transfer「移動」　■ Cuzco「クスコ〔11〜12世紀に建設されたインカ帝国の都市。世界遺産〕」
- Urubamba「ウルバンバ〔渓谷の町〕」　■ admission「入場(料)」

Travel

Airline

Hotel

Q1 How do the tourists get to Cuzco?

　a. By train

　b. By air

　c. By bus

Q2 What is NOT included in the price?

　a. Hotel charges

　b. Service charges

　c. Round-trip international airfare

Q3 If a couple is traveling together, how much would they pay for this tour?

　a. $1,095

　b. $1,745

　c. $2,190

Grand Canyon Vacation Tours Inc. Tour Cancellation Policy

Tours costing less than $500: Reservations under US$500 can be canceled anytime up to 48 hours prior to the departure for a full refund. Cancellations within the 48-hour period prior to the departure will receive a 50% refund. There is no refund for "no-shows"—failure to be at the correct pick-up location at the correct time.

Tours costing $500 or more: Tours costing a total of US$500 or more can be canceled up to 30 days prior to the departure for a full refund. Cancellations from 30 days to 48 hours prior to the departure will receive a 50% refund. There is no refund for cancellations within the 48-hour period prior to the departure. There is also no refund for "no-shows"—failure to be at the correct pick-up location at the correct time.

Please call us toll-free at 1-800-988-4289 if you have any questions. We look forward to seeing you at the Grand Canyon!

Vocabulary Notes ■ prior to… 「…の前に」 ■ full refund 「全額返金」 ■ toll-free 「フリーダイヤルで」

Q1 Complete the chart below.

Refund Policy				
Tour Price \ Time of Cancellation	Up to 30 days before	30 days–48 hrs before	48 hrs before departure	No-shows
Less than $500	100%			
$500 or more				No refund

Q2 What does "no-show" mean?

Traveling Further

Search for a tour itinerary on the Internet. Find out tour information such as destinations, price, duration, transportation, things included, etc. Report your findings in class.

Unit 3
Escorting a tour

ツアーコンダクター (tour leader) とは、ツアー参加者が出発から到着まで安全に楽しい旅を送ることができるように旅程中の実務を行い、旅の演出をも行う仕事です。英語力はもちろん旅行の実務知識、コミュニケーション力、トラブル時の判断力などさまざまな能力が関わってきます。

Warm-up

枠内のリストは、ツアーコンダクターがツアーに添乗する際に行う業務です。
業務の流れの順番に並べてみましょう。ペアまたはグループで答えを確認しましょう。

1. [a] ▶ 2. [ ] ▶ 3. [ ] ▶ 4. [ ] ▶ 5. [ ] ▶ 6. [ ] ▶ 7. [ ]

- **a.** Meet the group and greet them.
- **b.** Check the group in at the departure airport.
- **c.** Check the group in at the hotel.
- **d.** Check the group in for the return flight.
- **e.** After arrival, take the group to their hotel.
- **f.** Take the group on a sightseeing tour.
- **g.** Check the group out at the hotel.

Listening

ツアーコンダクター (女性) と客室乗務員 (男性)、ホテルのフロント係 (男性) のダイアログを聞いてみましょう。

 08

A Listen to the audio and check True or False.

[Scene 1] **1.** The sick passenger is in Seat 14C. ☐ True ☐ False

[Scene 2] **2.** Ms. Mizuno lost her camera. ☐ True ☐ False

3. The camera was left at around 8:30. ☐ True ☐ False

B Listen again and answer the following questions.

[Scene 1] **1.** What will the flight attendant bring when he comes back?

_____

2. What does the flight attendant ask the tour leader to do?

_____

[Scene 2] **3.** What is the lost camera like?

_____

Travel
Airline
Hotel

今度はダイアログを読んで、その内容を確認しましょう。
次に音声を聞きながら練習をし、ペアで読み合わせをしましょう。

08

[Scene 1: On a flight]

Tour leader: Excuse me. **One of my tour group members seems to** be suffering from **airsickness**. She is over there in Seat 40C.

Flight attendant: Oh, let me go and check on her.

Tour leader: Thank you. I'll come with you to **translate**.

Flight attendant: Are you OK, ma'am?

Tour leader: She says she needs some water and an extra **disposal bag**.

Flight attendant: Sure. I will be right back.

Tour leader: She is also asking if you have any medicine for airsickness.

Flight attendant: Yes, we do. I will get that, too. Please tell her to keep her seatbelt on as a precaution against sudden **turbulence**.

Tour leader: I will. Thank you for your help.

[Scene 2: At a hotel]

Front desk clerk: Hello. Front desk. May I help you?

Tour leader: Yes. I'm Ms. Mizuno, a tour leader, in Room 234. One of my tour members left her camera in the front lobby area this morning.

Front desk clerk: Let me check our **lost and found log**. Hold on a second, ma'am… I am afraid we have no record of a camera turned in yet. **Do you know what kind of camera it is?**

Tour leader: It is a Canon digital camera. It has a name tag with the name "Abe" in English.

Front desk clerk: I see. Around what time and where did she leave it?

Tour leader: She left it when she was sitting in the lobby after breakfast, around 8:30.

Front desk clerk: All right. I will keep this on record and make sure to call you if we have some information.

Tour leader: Thank you very much.

Vocabulary and Useful Expressions

tour leader	「ツアーコンダクター」 tour conductor でも意味は通じますが、あまり使用されません。tour guide とも呼びます。
One of my tour group members seems to…	「ツアー参加者の一人が…のようです」
airsickness	「航空機酔い、空酔い」 形容詞は airsick で be airsick、become airsick のように使います。
flight attendant	「飛行機の客室乗務員」 cabin crew とも呼びます。stewardess/steward と呼んだ時代もありましたが、男女同じ名称で呼ぶことを好む現在では使われません。
translate	「通訳する」
disposal bag	「〔飛行機のシートに備え付けてある〕ゴミ袋」 防水性の袋で、airsickness bag ともいいます。
turbulence	「乱気流」 precaution against sudden turbulence（突然の気流の変化に備えて）は機内アナウンスでよく使われるフレーズです。
lost and found	「遺失物」
log	「記録簿」= log book
Do you know what kind of camera it is?	「どのようなカメラかご存じですか」 間接疑問文です。疑問詞の後の主語・動詞の順に注意しましょう。

Travel

Airline

Hotel

Column

世界遺産 (World Heritage)

旅行の目的地 (destination) として今人気なのは、何といっても世界遺産を訪れる旅でしょう。パリに本部のある国連機関の UNESCO が世界遺産に関する活動の中心となっています。世界遺産には人類の歴史や地球の営みから生まれた貴重な文化財や自然環境があります。世界遺産条約に基づき、審査を経て UNESCO が世界遺産登録の認定を行います。毎年20件近くが新しく登録されてその数は増え、2017年には1千件を超えました。アンコールワットのように、内戦などにより崩壊の危機に瀕しながら危機遺産登録されて積極的に復興が行われたことにより、危機遺産ではなくなったケースもあります。

Pair Speaking Practice

A 病人について伝える練習をしましょう。

09

Tour leader: **One of my group members seems to** ¹be suffering from airsickness.

Flight attendant: Oh, let me ²go and check. Where is that person sitting?

Tour leader: He is over there in Seat ³45G.

	1	2	3
1st Time	be feverish	take his temperature	26F
2nd Time	have a stomachache	get some medicine	19B
3rd Time	feel very cold	get a blanket	37A

B 遺失物について伝える練習をしましょう。

10

Tour leader: One of my tour members has ¹lost her camera.

Front desk clerk: Oh, really? **Do you know** ²**what kind of camera it is?**

Tour leader: Yes, ³it's a Canon 7000.

	1	2	3
1st Time	lost his jacket	what color it is	it's light green
2nd Time	left her tablet in the lobby	where in the lobby she left it	on the sofa or the coffee table
3rd Time	found a wallet in the elevator	what time she found it	at around 8:00 a.m.

Role Play ツアー参加者の遺失物について問い合わせましょう。
必要なセリフをダイアログから抜き出して覚え、交替でロールプレイをしてみましょう。

Student A

You are a tour leader.
One of your tour members left his wallet at the hotel restaurant when he had breakfast this morning. Call the hotel front desk to try to find the wallet for your customer.

Student B

You are a hotel front desk clerk. You receive a call from a tour leader saying that his/her group member lost a wallet. You check your log book, but the wallet has not been turned in yet. Get information from the tour leader and tell him/her that you will call if it is found.

Topic Reading **1** 遊園地のサービスガイドを読んで、正誤問題に答えましょう。

Welcome to America's Greatest Theme Park!

Information Center

Our Information Center provides answers to your questions about the park and the local area. Stop by and let us help you to make your day more enjoyable!

Banking Services & Foreign Currency

Three ATMs are located in the park; see map for exact locations. At the Information Center, most major currencies can be exchanged for U.S. currency at current exchange rates. A small service fee applies.

First Aid

Our First Aid staff is on duty for the duration of the park's operating hours. Our office is located just across from Monster Ride. Notify any employee if you require First Aid assistance anywhere in the park.

Meeting Up

Out of consideration for all of our guests, we do not offer personal paging. We recommend that all members of your group know where and when to meet. If you become separated, you can leave a message at either our Lost Child Center in Center Square or the Information Center located at the Main Gate.

Lockers

A limited number of lockers is available across from Monster Ride, next to First Aid. Additional lockers are located by the restrooms near River Rapids.

Lost Child Center

Any child appearing to be lost will be taken to the Lost Child Center in Center Square. If you are separated from your child, ask any employee for assistance.

Vocabulary Notes   ▪ theme park「テーマパーク」   ▪ currency「貨幣、通貨」   ▪ exchange rate「外貨交換レート」
▪ on duty「職務にあたって」   ▪ paging「呼び出し」

1. First Aid is located next to Monster Ride.　□ True　□ False

2. Foreign currencies can be exchanged without any service charge.　□ True　□ False

3. If you are separated from your friend, you can ask for personal paging.　□ True　□ False

4. Lockers are available at two locations.　□ True　□ False

5. If your six-year-old sister gets lost, she will most likely be taken to the Information Center.　□ True　□ False

UNESCO World Heritage site: the Pyramid Fields

Three pyramids standing on the west bank of the Nile River near Giza, together with the other ancient ruins of the Memphis area, were designated a World Heritage site in 1979. They were constructed in the 25th century B.C. and have attracted many tourists since the Classical Period. According to Herodotus, a Greek historian in the fifth century B.C., about 100,000 people worked on the construction of the pyramids of Giza. It took 10 years to construct the road leading to the pyramids, and another 10 years to complete the pyramids themselves.

Pyramids were made as tombs for pharaohs. These pharaohs prepared for death: they tried to build a safe resting place to last an eternity. However, it did not always work as they wished. Often tomb robbers broke into the tombs and removed all the valuables, and even unwrapped mummies to steal jewelry from the dead.

These pyramids still hold a lot of secrets. It is not completely known yet how the heavy stones were carried and piled up. Some people say the pyramids are related to some lost culture, or even to aliens from outer space. It is said that the pyramids have mysterious power and there is strong magnetism and electric power inside them. Strangely, food does not spoil easily in the pyramids. These mysteries remain unexplained to this day.

Vocabulary Notes	■ bank 「川岸」　■ Giza 「ギザ〔カイロの南西に位置する町〕」　■ ruins 「遺跡」　■ designate 「指定する」 ■ Classical Period 「古代ギリシャ・ローマ時代」　■ pharaoh 「古代エジプト王の称号」 ■ mummy 「ミイラ」　■ magnetism 「磁気」　■ spoil 「腐る」

Q1 When did the pyramids of Giza become popular with tourists?

_____

Q2 What were the pyramids made for?

_____

Q3 What did the tomb robbers do?

_____

Q4 Why are the pyramids still mysterious?

_____

Traveling Further

What other World Heritage sites are there? Choose one heritage site of interest to you (or your group) and do research on it (location, history, features, etc.). Report the results to your classmates.

Welcoming international tourists

インバウンド客の急速な増加に伴い、日本全国各地の様々な観光地では外国語で対応できる観光ガイドの需要も高まるばかりです。ガイドの仕事は観光地の説明のみならず、日本の文化・歴史・地理など、英語力に加え幅広い知識が求められます。

Warm-up
日本の観光地についての問題に答えましょう。
そして、自分の答えをパートナーとシェアしましょう。

Q1 Think of two sightseeing spots you would recommend to international tourists.

Spot	1.	2.

Q2 Why would you recommend the spots?

Reason	1.	2.

Listening
バスツアーのガイド（女性）と乗客（男性）のダイアログを聞いてみましょう。

A Listen to the audio and check True or False.

1. The first stop of this tour is the Imperial Palace Plaza. ☐ True ☐ False
2. The tourists will have some free time to buy souvenirs. ☐ True ☐ False
3. The tourists can leave their bags and valuables on the bus. ☐ True ☐ False

B Listen again and answer the following questions.

1. How long does it take to the first stop?

2. Why is one of the passengers feeling very tired?

3. What is *shabu-shabu* like? Describe it.

[At the tour bus terminal]

Tour guide: Good morning. This is the bus for the **full-day tour** of the Greater Tokyo Metropolitan area. In about 10 minutes, we will be leaving, so please **check in** with me at the bus door now.

[After the **departure**]

Tour guide: Hello, everyone. My name is Misa Aso. I will be your guide today. **Please feel free to** ask any questions at any time. We are now heading toward our first stop of this tour, the **Imperial Palace** Plaza.

Tourist: Excuse me. How long does it take to the first stop?

Tour guide: **It takes** about 15 **minutes** or so.

Tourist: OK. I think I can stay awake until then. I feel very tired from **jet lag**.

Tour guide: Oh. I'm sorry to hear that, but I'm sure today's busy schedule will help you adjust to the **time difference**. Now, after the short walk around the palace, we will visit Asakusa Kannon, the oldest **Buddhist temple** in Tokyo. You will find many tiny shops where you can buy **souvenirs** in the arcade leading to the temple.

Tourist: Will we have some free time to do shopping there?

Tour guide: Yes, you will have half an hour to explore the area on your own. After the free time, you will have a *shabu-shabu* lunch at a restaurant nearby.

Tourist: What's *shabu-shabu*?

Tour guide: It's a popular kind of Japanese **cuisine**. You boil thinly sliced pieces of meat and vegetables in a hot pot in front of you.

Tourist: Sounds interesting.

Tour guide: Yes. I hope you will like it. Now, we will be arriving at the Imperial Palace shortly. It is the residence of the Japanese **Emperor** and…

Tourist: Excuse me, but are we going to enter the residence?

Tour guide: No, **I'm afraid we are not allowed to** go inside. Oh, we are here. You may leave your **luggage** on the bus, but please take your **valuables** with you.

Vocabulary and Useful Expressions

tour guide	「ツアーガイド」 訪日外国人のためのガイドは国家試験資格を持つ通訳案内士（通称：通訳ガイド）が活躍しています。2018年よりこの国家資格を持たなくても、報酬を得てガイドをすることが可能になりました。
full-day tour	「1日観光ツアー」 半日は half-day tour、1泊は overnight tour です。
check in	「チェックイン」 バスのチェックインとは名前を参加者リストと照らし合わせることです。
departure	「出発」↔ arrival
Please feel free to…	「ご自由に（遠慮なく）…してください」
Imperial Palace	「皇居」
It takes … minutes	「…分間かかります」
jet lag	「時差ぼけ」 have jet lag、suffer from jet lag のように使います。
time difference	「時差」
Buddhist temple	「仏教の寺」
souvenir	「お土産」
cuisine	「料理」 日本の料理を英語で説明できるようにしておくことが必要です。sukiyaki、sushi、sashimi、tempura、teriyaki、ramen などは英語として定着している日本料理名です。また海外からの旅行客の中には、宗教上の理由や個人的な信条により特定の食材を避けている場合やアレルギーを持っている場合があるので注意を払いましょう。
Emperor	「天皇」
I'm afraid we/you are not allowed to…	「あいにく…してはいけません」 You can't…と言うよりも丁寧で間接的なので、お客様に注意を与えるときなどに使うとよい表現です。 e.g. I'm afraid you are not allowed to take pictures here.
luggage	「荷物」= baggage
valuables	「貴重品」

Travel

Airline 　Hotel

Column

時差ぼけ解消法

時差ぼけは、出発地点から5時間以上の時差がある場所で症状が出始めるとされています。太陽に逆らって飛ぶ東行き（米国方面など）の方が西行き（EU方面など）よりも症状が重いのが普通です。寝付けない、寝付いても途中で眼が覚めるというのが、旅人を最も悩ませる症状です。また、倦怠感や食欲不振などが出ることもあります。対処法としては、機内で目的地時間に合わせて過ごすこと（到着が夜なら睡眠はとらないなど）、到着後は日中十分に日光を浴びることが大事です。日光は体内時計をリセットする働きをします。

Pair Speaking Practice

A 以下の会話を練習しましょう。

> Tourist:　How long does it take to ¹go to the palace from here?
>
> Tour guide:　**It takes about** ²15 minutes.

	1	2
1st Time	go to downtown Tokyo from Narita Airport	an hour and a half
2nd Time	fly to Bangkok from Osaka Itami Airport	six hours
3rd Time	walk to the top of Mt. Fuji from the 5th station	seven hours

B 旅行客からの質問に対し、I'm afraid you are not allowed to...という表現を使い、
「それはあいにくできません」という申し訳ない気持ちを伝えましょう。

> Tourist:　Can I ¹take pictures here?
>
> Tour guide:　**I'm afraid you are not allowed to** ²take pictures here.

	1	2
1st Time	videotape the play	videotape the play
2nd Time	throw away these bottles in this box	throw away these bottles in this box
3rd Time	go in there with my shoes on	go in there with your shoes on

Role Play　訪日した外国人客に、通訳ガイドとして対応する練習をしましょう。
必要なセリフをダイアログから抜き出して覚え、交替でロールプレイをしてみましょう。

Student A

You are a tour guide. Greet your bus passengers and tell them today's schedule. Look at your memo below and answer your passenger's questions.

Student B

You are a tourist on a tour bus. Ask your guide questions from your brochure. Your questions are listed below.

\<Job Memo\>

- 5/20 (Wed)
- 12 passengers reserved

Tokyo half-day tour (9:00–12:00)

1. Tokyo Tower [go to the top] (20 min.)
→ 2. Odaiba (free time 30 min.)
→ 3. Sumida River cruise (30 min.)
→ 4. Asakusa (end)

- No lunch

Highlights of Tokyo in just half a day!

Great bus tour!
  `Free time?`

Visit Tokyo Tower and popular Odaiba.

Enjoy a Sumida River cruise. `How long?`

The tour ends in Asakusa. `End time?`

Explore the area to your heart's content!
  `Lunch?`

32

Topic Reading 1 JRからの外国人旅行者のための情報を読んで、正誤問題に答えましょう。

JR (Japan Railway) Group offers an economical and convenient railway pass to travelers from foreign countries. Below is some information about the pass.

Japan Rail Pass Information

Eligible traveler:	Foreign nationals visiting Japan with the entry status of Temporary Visitor.
Description:	■ All JR Group Railways, Shinkansen "bullet trains" (except any reserved or non-reserved seat on "Nozomi" and "Mizuho" trains), limited express trains, express trains, and rapid or local trains. ■ Local lines of JR Bus (excluding some lines) ■ Buy your Exchange Order for the Japan Rail Pass at sales offices or agents before coming to Japan. After you arrive in Japan, turn in your Exchange Order to receive your pass at a major JR station.
Valid period and prices (Child fare & Green Seat Pass also available):	▸ 7 days: 29,110 yen ▸ 14 days: 46,390 yen ▸ 21 days: 59,350 yen
How to use It:	■ When you begin using your pass, present it to the attendant at a manned ticket gate. The attendant will apply a stamp for official use. When passing through the gate, always present your pass to the attendant so that the period of validity is visible. ■ While using your pass, you must carry your passport and be prepared to present it to a station attendant or car conductor if requested.

Vocabulary Notes
- eligible「資格のある」 ■ Temporary Visitor「一時滞在者〔旅行者のように居住目的でない訪問者〕」
- exchange order「引換証〔XOと略すこともある〕」 ■ valid「有効な」
- manned ticket gate「駅員のいる改札」 ■ validity「有効」

Travel
Airline
Hotel

1. People from foreign countries living in Japan can't use this pass. ☐ True ☐ False
2. Eligible travelers can use any JR trains including all Shinkansen trains. ☐ True ☐ False
3. Eligible travelers can buy this pass at a major JR station. ☐ True ☐ False
4. Eligible travelers will receive a stamp when they first start using it. ☐ True ☐ False

One Day Tokyo Shitamachi Tour

Greetings from your tour guide: Hello! My name is Hiroko. I'm a national licensed tour guide and interpreter, living in Tokyo, Japan. I have guided tourists from overseas for more than 8 years now. My major was Japanese history and I am sure my guided tour can fully satisfy you and make you want to come back to Japan! I am looking forward to traveling with you.

My tour: My tour begins in the shitamachi area of Nezu and ends in Asakusa. Here we discover the sights that the common people of Edo loved to visit.

Itinerary: Nezu Jinja ▶ Sendagi ▶ Yanaka Ginza High Street ▶ Yanaka Cemetary ▶ Tenno-ji ▶ Ueno Park–Saigo Takamori ▶ Okachimachi–Ameyoko ▶ Asakusa

Meeting location: Will meet at your hotel / **Duration:** 7 hours (full day)

Transportation: Public transportation plus lots of walking

Tour fee and what's included: 30,000 yen (All transfers from hotel to sites on itinerary and entrance fees where applicable)

Contact: hiroguide@guideguide.com

Vocabulary Notes
- interpreter「通訳」 - where applicable「該当する場合」

Q1 What do you think are the best points of this guide?

_____

Q2 What do you think are the best points of this tour?

_____

Q3 What is covered by the tour fee?

_____

Traveling Further

Choose one sightseeing spot in Japan and prepare to guide your international guests around there. Practice describing the spot without reading a script, and act out your tour in class.

Taking an airline reservation

航空会社には予約や問い合わせの電話が終日かかってきます。フライト情報、空席情報、予約など、会話の内容には一定のパターンがあります。代表的なパターンを覚えて練習しましょう。

Travel Airline Hotel

Warm-up 次の問題に答えましょう。

Q1 You work at an airline reservation center and you are receiving a flight reservation from a customer. What information do you need to get from the customer? List the items.

_____

_____

Q2 Read the following numbers and write them down as you would say them. 🎧 14

1. (Tel.) 03-865-7900 _____
2. 9:45 p.m. _____
3. 8:05 a.m. _____
4. Dec. 12 _____
5. Flight 203 _____

Listening 航空会社の予約係（女性）とお客様（男性）の電話でのダイアログを聞いてみましょう。 🎧 15

A Listen to the audio and check True or False.

1. The caller wants to go to Paris on Saturday. ☐ True ☐ False
2. There are three flights to Paris on that day. ☐ True ☐ False
3. The caller wants to be back on September 20. ☐ True ☐ False

B Listen again and answer the following questions.

1. What is the caller's last name? _____
2. What time does his flight to Paris leave from Narita? _____
3. On what date does his return flight leave for Narita? _____

35

[At an airline office]

Reservation clerk: Hello, ABC Airlines. This is Ms. Tanaka speaking. How may I help you?

Caller: I'd like to fly business **class** to Paris on Sunday, September 8. What flights do you have?

Reservation clerk: Let me check... Yes, sir, we have a **direct flight** at 11:30 a.m. and another direct flight at 7:30 p.m. **Which would you prefer?**

Caller: I prefer the morning flight. Can you put me on that flight?

Reservation clerk: Let me check the **availability**...
Yes, I can put you in business class. How about the return flight?

Caller: I need to come back on September 20.

Reservation clerk: Flight 204 leaves Paris at 1:10 p.m. on the 19th and arrives at Narita at 10:15 a.m. on the next day. How does that sound?

Caller: Sounds fine.

Reservation clerk: Good. Let me book the flights for you. **May I have your name, please?**

Caller: David Shapell.

Reservation clerk: **Would you spell out your last name, please?**

Caller: It's S-H-A-P-E-L-L.

Reservation clerk: Thank you, Mr. Shapell. May I have your contact number?

Caller: Sure. My office number is 024-348-2908.

Reservation clerk: 024-348-2908. So you have a reservation on Flight 203 leaving Narita at 11:30 a.m. on September 8, arriving at **Charles de Gaulle Airport** at 4:40 p.m. on the same day. Your return flight, 204, leaves Paris at 1:10 p.m. on the 19th of September, and arrives at Narita at 10:15 a.m. on the 20th.

Caller: OK. Very good.

Reservation clerk: Now, your **reservation number** is 4, **B for baker**, A for able, 55. That's 4BA55.

Caller: 4BA55. Thank you very much.

Reservation clerk: Thank you, Mr. Shapell.

Vocabulary and Useful Expressions

class	「クラス」 多くのフライトではファーストクラス、ビジネスクラス、エコノミークラスの3つに分かれていますが、行き先によっては2クラスのみ、またはオールエコノミーの場合もあります。シートの大きさとゆとり、食事、荷物の許容量などのサービス内容の違いがあります。
direct flight	「直行便」 non-stop flight ともいいます。途中寄港があるのは stopover です。
Which would you prefer?	「どちらがよろしいでしょうか」
availability	「空席状況」
May I have your name, please?	「お名前を伺ってもよろしいでしょうか」 What's your name? の丁寧な言い方です。May I have...? で相手の情報を丁寧に聞くことができきます。
Would you spell out your last name, please?	「名字のつづりをお願いできますか」 外国名は聞き慣れていないので、スペルを言ってもらうのが確実です。Would you...? は丁寧にお願いする言い方です。
Charles de Gaulle Airport	「シャルルドゴール空港」 パリの国際空港の名称。略号は CDG。各空港には3文字のアルファベットのエアポートコードが割り当てられています。104ページを参照。
reservation number	「予約番号」 reference number ともいい、予約を入れたときに後の確認のためにコンピュータに登録する番号。通常アルファベットと数字の混合した記号である場合が多いようです。
B for baker	「baker の B」 お客様の名前や住所などのスペルは D と B や M と N の聞き違いなど電話上ではミスが起こりがちです。確認のために使用されるのが通話コードです。103ページにある Appendix 2の2例は tourism で使われる頻度の高いものです。for の代わりに as in を使用することもあります。 e.g. "Ms. Chen, let me confirm your last name—C, H, E for easy, N for Nancy. Correct?"

Travel

Airline

Hotel

Column

旅客機

現在の旅客機の主流はボーイング777や787などで、250人ほど搭乗できる中型の飛行機です。以前は国内線では500人以上を乗せることもできる2階建てのジャンボ機（ボーイング747）が主流の時代もありました。しかし、航空輸送のニーズが拡大する中、効率や小回りが重視され、航空会社の運行効率を上げるため、取り回しの良い中型機や小型機が好まれるようになったのです。それにしても、飛行機のような大きな鉄の塊が空へ飛び立てることが不思議と思う人も多いでしょう。これは強力なジェットエンジンと翼が前方から風を受けたときに生じる揚力作用によるのです。ところで、飛行機の翼が燃料タンクであることはご存じでしたか？

Pair Speaking Practice

A パートナーにどちらが好みかを聞き、相手の答えに対して "Why?" と尋ねてみましょう。

Which would you prefer, _____?

1st Time	beef or chicken	3rd Time	a window seat or an aisle seat
2nd Time	white wine or red wine	4th Time	*think of your own*

B お客様の名前を聞く練習をしましょう。

Reservation clerk:	*(ask your partner's name politely)*
Customer:	*(say your name)*
Reservation clerk:	*(ask how to spell it)*
Customer:	*(give the spelling)*

C 103ページの通信コード (Phonetic Codes) を使って、次の予約番号を伝えましょう。

A: Your reservation number is _____.

B: Pardon me?

A: *(use phonetic codes)*

1st Time	MNX67P	3rd Time	CDTP43
2nd Time	TR987B	4th Time	*think of your own*

Role Play 予約の電話を受けましょう。
必要なセリフをダイアログから抜き出して覚え、交替でロールプレイをしてみましょう。

Student A

You are a customer. You plan to fly to Los Angeles. Call the airline and make a reservation. Here is your schedule.

July 25	Leave for Los Angeles (LAX)
August 5	Arrive back in Tokyo (NRT)

Student B

You are an airline reservation clerk. Take the customer's reservation. You have the following information.

Destination	Flight number	Day	Departure	Arrival
Flight to Los Angeles (LAX)	NH006	daily	4:00 p.m.	10:05 a.m.
	NH018	daily	5:05 p.m.	11:10 a.m.
Flight to Tokyo (NRT)	NH005	daily	11:40 a.m.	3:05 p.m. (next day)
	NH019	daily	12:55 p.m.	4:20 p.m. (next day)

Topic Reading 1 予約と支払いに関する情報を読んで、質問に答えましょう。

ABC Airlines Booking and Payment

Book your flight through the ABC Airlines website. You can select your flights and dates and pay efficiently with the click of a mouse. You have payment options of credit or debit cards and online payment services like Apple Pay or PayPal. We make sure all your personal information and payments are secured and protected.

If your online payment was successful but you do not receive our confirmation within an hour, please contact our Customer Service Center. For details about refunds of purchases made through our website, please see our Guidelines for Payments web page. All refunds will be processed to the same card used to make the booking.

Vocabulary Notes ■ confirmation「確認」 ■ refund「返金」 ■ purchase「購入」

Q1 What methods of payment are available when you book a flight through this website?

Q2 What should you do if you don't get any confirmation on your payment?

Q3 If you need to cancel the online reservation and find out how to get your money back, what should you do?

Q4 What is the main purpose of this website?

ABC Airlines Flight Attendant: Online application now open

ABC Airlines now welcomes individuals who are customer-orientated and team players to join us as flight attendants. Applicants should have strong interpersonal communication skills and the ability to deal with people from different cultures. If you meet the following requirements, we will be pleased to meet you for an interview:

- Minimum age of 20 years old
- Minimum height requirement of at least 1.57 m (in order to reach safety equipment)
- Junior college or University degree holder
- High level of English proficiency (additional languages are desirable)
- Willing to be based in the U.S.

Online applications for this year are now being accepted. As we accept applications on a rolling basis, we encourage you to apply soon. Shortlisted applicants will be invited to submit a video self-introduction online.

Vocabulary Notes
- application「申込み」 ■ requirements「条件」 ■ on a rolling basis「順次」
- shortlisted applicants「選考に残った応募者」

Q1 What kind of character are the flight attendants expected to have?

_____

Q2 What kind of physical requirements are set for the flight attendants?

_____

Q3 After receiving the online application from you, what will the Airlines do?

_____

Traveling Further

There are many airlines in the world. Pick one airline company from any country of the world. Find their website and get information about the airline (logo mark, areas of operation, features, uniforms of flight attendants, etc.). Share your findings with your classmates.

Unit 6

Giving flight information

お客様からの質問は、フライトの情報・予約・キャンセルについてはもちろん、機内サービスやマイレージプログラムについて、さらには入国・通関情報や時差についてなど、多岐にわたります。このような質問に迅速に正確に答えられるよう、知識を頭に入れ、常に資料を整理しておくことが必要です。

Travel
Airline
Hotel

Warm-up pp. 6–7のタイムゾーンマップ (Standard Time Zones of the World) を見て答えましょう。

Q1 What is the time difference between the following cities?

1. Tokyo and Beijing? [It is one hour.]
2. New York and Los Angeles? [   ]
3. Sydney and Tokyo? [   ]
4. Osaka and London? [   ]

Q2 Look at the time and date in London (UTC Zone). Fill in the time and date in each city.

London [0:00 Jan. 1] **Tokyo** [   ] **New York** [   ] **Bangkok** [   ]

Listening 航空便の予約担当者 (男性) とお客様 (女性) のダイアログを聞いてみましょう。

A Listen to the audio and check True or False.

1. The caller wants to change her reservation to the next day. ☐ True ☐ False
2. The caller would like to be put on the waiting list. ☐ True ☐ False
3. The caller ordered a vegetarian meal. ☐ True ☐ False

B Listen again and answer the following questions.

1. What is the caller's reservation number? _____
2. What time does her flight arrive in Manila? _____
3. What meal service will be offered on this flight? _____

41

[At an airline office]

Reservation clerk: Good morning, ABC Airlines. How may I help you?

Caller: Hello. I have a flight reservation from Tokyo to Manila. Is it possible to change the date?

Reservation clerk: If seats are **available**, yes. Do you have your reservation number?

Caller: Yes, it's 246CFK.

Reservation clerk: Thank you… **Ms.** Hong? Your reservation is for Flight 837 to Manila on May 21?

Caller: That's right, and I would like to change it to the day before. Do you have the same flight on that day?

Reservation clerk: Yes, 837 is a **daily flight**. Let me check now… Ms. Hong, I'm afraid that flight is already **full**. Would you like to be on the **waiting list**?

Caller: Yes, please.

Reservation clerk: All right. We'll give you a call if a seat becomes available.

Caller: Thank you. Is there a time difference between Tokyo and Manila?

Reservation clerk: Yes, there is a one-hour time difference. Manila is **one hour behind**.

Caller: I see. My arrival time is 3:30, but is this local time or Tokyo time?

Reservation clerk: It is Manila time, madam.

Caller: OK. By the way, do you have **meal service** on this flight?

Reservation clerk: Yes, madam. There'll be a lunch service.

Caller: Do you serve **special meals** for vegetarians? I'm vegetarian.

Reservation clerk: Yes, we do. I'll order a vegetarian meal for you.

Caller: Thank you.

Reservation clerk: **Is there anything else I can help you with**, Ms. Hong**?**

Caller: No, that's all. Thank you very much.

Vocabulary and Useful Expressions

available	「利用可能な」 名詞形は availability (→ Unit 5) です。
Ms. …	「…さん」 相手が女性で既婚か未婚か不明な場合は Ms.[miz] を使用します。
daily flight	「毎日運行する便」
full	「満席で」 「満席の便」は full flight です。
waiting list	「フライトを予約する順番待ちのために名前を載せるリスト」 他の搭乗予定者のキャンセル (cancellation) が出るとリストの上の人からフライトの予約ができます。Put me on the waiting list. のように〈put ＋人＋ on〉、または I want to get on the waiting list. のように get on を使用します。
one hour behind	「1時間遅れ」 逆に進んでいる場合は ahead (of) で表現します。あとに都市名が来る場合は次のようになります。 e.g. Tokyo is 9 hours ahead of London. / London is 9 hours behind Tokyo.
meal service	「(機内の) 食事サービス」
special meal	「特別食」 機内の食事サービスには子供用 (child meal)、菜食主義者のための vegetarian meal、その他宗教的な理由による特別食 (ヒンズー教徒用のビーフ抜きの食事、イスラム教徒用のポーク抜きの食事)、アレルギーや糖尿病など疾患のある人のための特別食などがあり、いずれも予約時に注文できます。
Is there anything else I can help you with?	「ほかにご用はございませんか」 お客様への対応が終わったことを確認するときのフレーズです。

Travel　Airline　Hotel

Column

時差の計算

時差はややこしいイメージですが、その理論を理解するとそれほど複雑ではありません。経度0度のイギリスのグリニッジ天文台の子午線を基準として世界時が設定されていますが、これをセシウム原子時計によって正確に調整した協定世界時 (UTC=Coordinated Universal Time) が世界の標準時となっています。右の図は地球を真上から見たものです。UTC を基点として左右に12時間の時差が刻まれています。地球ひと回りで1日24時間となります。±12時間の地点に日付変更線 (International Date Line) があります。

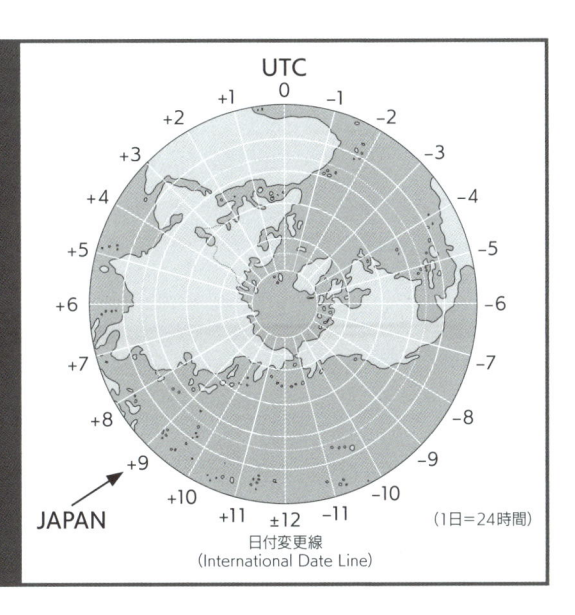

Pair Speaking Practice

A お客様の質問に答え、対応が終わったことを確認しましょう。 🎧 17

Caller:	[1]Do you have meal service on this flight?
Reservation clerk:	[2]Yes, we have lunch service.
Caller:	OK. Thank you.
Reservation clerk:	**Is there anything else I can help you with?**
Caller:	No, that's all. Thank you.

	1	2
1st Time	Is there a time difference between Tokyo and Seoul?	No, there isn't.
2nd Time	Is this a daily flight?	Yes, this is a daily flight.
3rd Time	Is this local time or Tokyo time?	It is local time.

B pp. 6–7のタイムゾーンマップ (Standard Time Zones of the World) から都市を2つ選び (下線部1と2)、時差を答える (下線部3) 練習をしましょう。

Caller: Is there a time difference between [1]_____ and [2]_____?

Reservation clerk: Yes, [1]_____ is [3]_____ **hour(s) ahead of/behind** [2]_____.

Role Play お客様が予約の変更をしたいと申し出ています。
必要なセリフをダイアログから抜き出して覚え、交替でロールプレイをしてみましょう。

Student A
You are a customer. You want to change your flight reservation to the next day, Tuesday, August 11. Your reservation number is 453B34.

Student B
You are an airline reservation clerk. You try to change your customer's reservation, but the flight is full. You can put him/her on the waiting list or recommend other flights.

Reservation Record

Reservation   #453B34
Mr./Ms. *your partner's name*
NH573 FUK-PEK   Aug 10 (Mon)   OK
NH574 PEK-FUK   Aug 16 (Sun)   OK

Timetable

NH573 (Mon, Tue, Sat)   15:10 福岡 – 18:30 北京
NH171 (Daily)   07:15 福岡 – 08:15 大阪
NH159 (Daily)   10:00 大阪 – 12:30 北京

注：FUK = 福岡   PEK = Beijing (北京)

44

Topic Reading 1 次の e-ticket を見て、質問に答えましょう。

ELECTRONIC TICKET ITINERARY/RECEIPT

ABC e-Tickets

Thank you for choosing ABC Airlines Electronic Tickets!
Your electronic airline ticket is stored in our computer system. As with all airline tickets, your electronic airline ticket is not transferable. When checking in at the airport, please present all necessary, country-specific travel documentation, this Itinerary/Receipt, and identification such as a passport. This Itinerary/Receipt must be presented at Immigration/Customs if requested.

FARE/TICKET INFORMATION

Passenger Name: Ms. Stacy Ford **Reservation No.:** REGJ74 **Date of Issue:** 28 MAR 19
Ticket Number: 2052101257060 **Fare:** JPY100,200 **Form of Payment:** Visa

ITINERARY

CITY	DATE	TIME	FLT NO	CLASS	STATUS	FLIGHT TIME
TOKYO	04 APR 19	1710	AC008	Y	OK	10 hrs. 00 min
SEATTLE	04 APR 19	1010	**Operating Carrier:** ABC AIRLINES			
SEATTLE	08 APR 19	1225	AC007	Y	OK	11 hrs. 00 min
TOKYO	09 APR 19	1625	**Operating Carrier:** ABC AIRLINES			

* The ticketing information contained in the ABC Airlines computer system shall prevail if there is any discrepancy between this Itinerary/Receipt and the ticketing information in our computer system.

Vocabulary Notes
- e-ticket「電子航空券〔航空券の情報が航空会社のシステムに記録されている〕」 ■ transferable「譲渡可能な」
- country-specific「その国特有の」 ■ JPY = Japanese yen
- Y「エコノミークラスを示す記号〔ビジネス C、ファースト F〕」 ■ prevail「優先する」 ■ discrepancy「不一致」

Travel

Airline

Hotel

Q1 Which of the following is true?

a. This e-ticket can be sold to someone else.

b. This e-ticket may be needed at immigration.

c. This e-ticket may be used as your identification.

Q2 How long does it take to fly from Tokyo to Seattle?

a. 5 hours

b. 10 hours

c. 11.5 hours

Q3 If the information on this e-ticket and on the airline's computer system is different, which is considered to be correct?

a. This e-ticket

b. The information on the airline's computer system

c. Neither

March 8, 2019

Dear Mr. Sato,

Welcome to our program! Thank you for becoming an ABCFlyers member. Your frequent flyer membership card is enclosed.

Now you can earn miles every time you fly with us. You will also earn miles by using ABCFlyers program partner hotels, car rental agencies and retail businesses. Soon you will have enough miles for your first travel award. For a complete listing of ABCFlyers program partners, please visit our website at www.abcflyers.com/member. You can redeem your miles on flights to over 300 cities in over 100 countries. Award levels start at just 5,000 miles for a one-class upgrade. For examples of how to use your miles to fly to other world destinations, please visit our website.

The ABCFlyers website is the most convenient way to track your miles and make the most of your membership. We invite you to sign up in order to receive monthly mileage summaries and our special promotions by email.

Once again, welcome to the ABCFlyers program. We look forward to having you fly with us soon.

Sincerely,

Jacob Perata

Jacob Perata, Chief Director
ABCFlyers Marketing Programs

Vocabulary Notes
- frequent flyer「（航空会社の）お得意様」 ■ enclose「同封する」 ■ earn「稼ぐ」
- redeem「引き換える」 ■ summary「集計」 ■ promotion「キャンペーン」

Q1 What was sent with this letter?

_____

Q2 How can Mr. Sato earn miles other than by flying with ABC Airlines?

_____

Q3 Where can Mr. Sato use his miles?

_____

Q4 In order to receive monthly mileage summaries, what should Mr. Sato do?

_____

Traveling Further

Choose one airline company and find out about its frequent flyer program. What is the name of the program? How can you earn mileage? What can you use the mileage for?

Helping passengers check in

空港のチェックインカウンターでは、フライト前の短時間に大勢のお客様に対処しなくてはなりません。時間帯によってはチェックイン待ちの長い列ができることもあります。多忙なときは事務的になりがちですが、余裕ある笑顔でお客様を送り出したいものです。

Warm-up 以下の問題に答えましょう。

Q1 Match the signs with the descriptions (a–f).

- **a.** You can buy things without paying tax here.
- **b.** Where the airplane departs from
- **c.** Your carry-on bags are checked here.
- **d.** You can get your boarding pass here.
- **e.** Show your passport here and get the date stamped on it.
- **f.** You have to say goodbye to your friends here.

Security Checkpoints ☐
Immigration ☐
Boarding Gate ☐
Departing Passengers Only ☐
Duty-free Shops ☐
Check-in Counter ☐

Q2 Put the signs in the order you will see them when departing from an international airport.

1. [Check-in Counter] ▶ **2.** [ ]
▶ **3.** [ ] ▶ **4.** [ ]
▶ **5.** [ ] ▶ **6.** [ ]

Listening チェックインカウンターでの係員（女性）と乗客（男性）のダイアログを聞いてみましょう。 🎧 18

A Listen to the audio and check True or False.

1. The passenger is flying to Frankfurt. ☐ True ☐ False
2. The passenger wants a window seat. ☐ True ☐ False
3. The passenger's seat number is 16A. ☐ True ☐ False

B Listen again and answer the following questions.

1. Who packed Mr. Bates's luggage? _____
2. Where is the baggage claim tag? _____
3. What time is boarding? _____

Travel · Airline · Hotel

[At the airline check-in counter]

Check-in clerk: Good morning! May I see your **ticket** and passport, please?

Passenger: Sure. Here you are.

Check-in clerk: Thank you, sir... You are **flying to** Frankfurt **via** Berlin. Would you like an **aisle seat** or a **window seat**?

Passenger: I'd like an aisle seat, please.

Check-in clerk: All right. Are you **checking in** any **luggage**?

Passenger: Yes, one suitcase.

Check-in clerk: **Could you** put your luggage on the scales**, please?**

Passenger: OK.

Check-in clerk: Thank you. I'd like to ask you a couple of **security questions**, sir. Did you pack your luggage by yourself?

Passenger: Yes, I did.

Check-in clerk: Have you left your luggage anywhere unattended?

Passenger: No, I haven't.

Check-in clerk: Thank you. Mr. Bates, **here is** your passport and **boarding pass**. Your seat number is 60A. Your luggage is **checked through to** Frankfurt.

Passenger: OK. Does that mean I don't have to worry about my luggage at Berlin?

Check-in clerk: That's right. There is a **baggage claim tag** on the back of the boarding pass. The **boarding time** is 9:30. **Please be sure to** be at Gate 11 before that.

Passenger: OK, thank you.

Check-in clerk: You're welcome. Enjoy your flight.

Vocabulary and Useful Expressions

ticket	「航空券」 正式には airline ticket です。席を購入した際に航空会社や旅行会社が発行し、予約内容や搭乗者の名前や支払い内容が記載されています。決済した後に入手するデータ（e チケット）をオンライン上に保存または印刷しておき、搭乗当日に搭乗券に交換します。
flying to A via B	「B（地名）経由でA（地名）へ行く」= through (thru) / by way of
aisle/window seat	「通路側／窓側の席」 予約時に seat request ができます。
check in luggage	「手荷物を受託する」 checked-in luggage は「受託手荷物」。名詞形は check-in とハイフンでつなげます。 e.g. Don't be late for check-in time.
Could you…, please?	「…していただけますか」 Unit 5で学習した would you…? 同様、丁寧に頼むときの言い方です。
security questions	「保安上の質問」 飛行機を安全に運行するため、このような質問をすることがあります。要人の利用や警戒すべき情報などにより security level は上下します。
here is…	「…をどうぞ」 人に物を渡すときの表現です。
boarding pass	「搭乗券」 飛行機に乗るための券で、チェックイン時に航空券を示して交換します。あるいは、事前のオンラインチェックインで自分で印刷または端末に保存して、持参します。ゲートや座席ナンバーや登場時刻の記載があります。
checked through to A	「荷物が経由地を通過して地点Aまで届けられる」
baggage claim tag	「手荷物受領証」 baggage claim は「荷物引き取り所」という意味。
boarding time	「搭乗時刻」 boarding は「搭乗」という意味。
Please be sure to…	「必ず…してください」

Travel Airline Hotel

Column

複数の空港

国際空港は海外の玄関口とも言え、その独特な雰囲気にわくわくする人は多いことでしょう。大都市にはいくつかの空港が存在することがあります。東京では成田と羽田、大阪では関西国際と伊丹とそれぞれ２つの空港があります。ニューヨーク近郊ではJFK（ジョンエフケネディー）、LGA（ラガーディア）、NWA（ニューワーク）の３つの空港が存在します。国際線と国内線の利用が分かれていたり、エアラインによって乗り入れる空港が異なる場合もあります。乗継ぐ際に同じ空港ではなく、違う空港に移動する場合もあります。案内の際には十分注意を払わなければなりません。

Pair Speaking Practice

A Could you..., please? を使ってお客様に丁寧な依頼をしてみましょう。  19

Check-in clerk: **Could you** [1]put your luggage on the scales**, please?**

Passenger: [2]All right.

	1	2
1st Time	go to your gate now	Sure.
2nd Time	show me your passport	Yes. Here you are.
3rd Time	sign here	OK. Here you go.

B Please be sure to...という表現を使って「必ず…するように」とお願いしましょう。 20

Check-in clerk: **Please be sure to** [1]be at Gate 11 before your boarding time.

Passenger: OK. I will be sure to [2]be there before my boarding time.

	1	2
1st Time	keep this claim tag	keep it
2nd Time	take your computer out of your bag	take it out of my bag
3rd Time	finish your drink before the security checkpoint	finish it before the checkpoint

Role Play チェックインするお客様に対応しましょう。
必要なセリフをダイアログから抜き出して覚え、交替でロールプレイをしてみましょう。

Student A

You are a passenger checking in to fly to Bangkok. You have one suitcase to check in.

Student B

You are an airline clerk checking a passenger in. You need to check his/her passport and airline ticket. Check his/her baggage in and give him/her the things he/she needs.

Seat Chart ✕…reserved

	A	B	C		D	E	F	G		H	K
26	✕	B	C	aisle	✕	✕	F	G	aisle	✕	K
27	✕	B	✕	aisle	✕	E	F	G	aisle	✕	K

Boarding Pass

NRT – BKK   Seat No. _____

Mr./Ms. *your partner's name*   Boarding Time   10:40 a.m.

Gate No. 18

注：BKK = Bangkok (バンコク)

Topic Reading 1 荷物の許容範囲に関する説明書きを読んで、質問に答えましょう。

Carry-on luggage policy   ABC Airlines

Maximum size: 35.5 cm × 56 cm × 23 cm

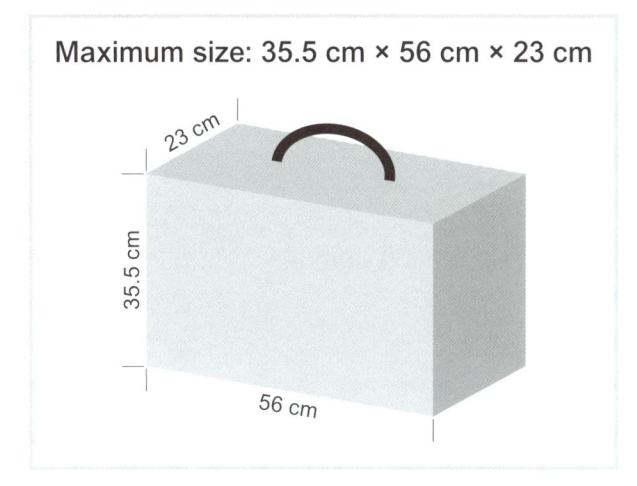

Each passenger is permitted to take one piece of carry-on luggage on board. It must fit in a carry-on sizing box, and maximum carry-on weight is 18 kg.

In addition, each passenger may carry one purse, briefcase or laptop computer. You may carry a small musical instrument or sports equipment on board as part of your carry-on baggage allowance as long as it is in a protective case and fits in the overhead storage bin.

First Class and Business Class passengers are allowed one additional piece of carry-on luggage. Each passenger is also allowed special items such as a coat, umbrella, cane, reading material and camera.

Please try to minimize the amount of carry-on luggage so that you may enjoy a more comfortable flight. For the sake of safety, please store your luggage under the seat in front of you or in the overhead storage bin. Baggage which cannot be accommodated in these spaces should be checked in.

Vocabulary Notes
- carry-on luggage 「機内持ち込み手荷物」 ■ sizing box 「サイズ計測箱」
- storage bin 「荷物入れ」 ■ accommodate 「収納する」

Travel | Airline | Hotel

Q1 If you are flying economy class, which items are you allowed to carry on board?

a. Two pieces of luggage
b. One small suitcase of 22 kg and a laptop computer bag
c. One 15 kg suitcase, one purse and camera

Q2 According to the description, which one of the following is correct?

a. You can carry your surfboard in a cabin as long as it is covered in a special case.
b. You should put your trumpet in a hard container if you want to take it on board.
c. You can take your violin on board if you pay a special fee.

Q3 According to the description, which of the following is correct?

a. You must check in baggage that exceeds the size limit.
b. You are advised to carry fewer items on board for your safety.
c. You should keep your luggage under your seat during take-off and landing.

ABC Airlines Online Check-in

The easiest way to check in!

Whether you are at home or outside, you can check in online on your computer, tablet or smartphone at abcairlines.com. Online check-in opens 24 hours before departure. You can get your boarding pass in just a few steps.

Step 1: Log in to abcairlines.com with your name and reservation number.
Step 2: Click "check-in."
Step 3: View your seat assignment and change if necessary.
Step 4: Click "confirm" and you're checked in.
Step 5: Print your boarding pass or receive it on your mobile device by email.

When you arrive at the airport, please proceed to a special baggage drop-off counter. If you only have carry-on baggage, go directly to the gate of your flight.

Vocabulary Notes ■ seat assignment「座席指定」 ■ proceed「進む」

Q1 In order to check in online, what do you need to have with you?

Q2 When can you start checking in online?

Q3 If you plan to check baggage in, where should you go at the airport?

Q4 What do you think are the advantages of online check-in?

Traveling Further

There are many people working at airports. What kinds of jobs are there? Find out about several different airport jobs and their responsibilities. Report your findings in class.

Unit 8

Working at the boarding gate

搭乗ゲートでは、いよいよこれから飛行機の旅に出る人々が期待や不安を抱いて出発を待っています。スムーズに空の旅へとご案内したいものですが、飛行機の遅れやトラブルがあれば、ここでお客様に説明し、適切に対処することが必要となります。

Warm-up 国際線のカウンターでは必ずパスポートをチェックし、本人確認を行います。
図はアメリカ人搭乗客のパスポートの1ページです。適切なものを枠内から選択して空欄を埋めましょう。

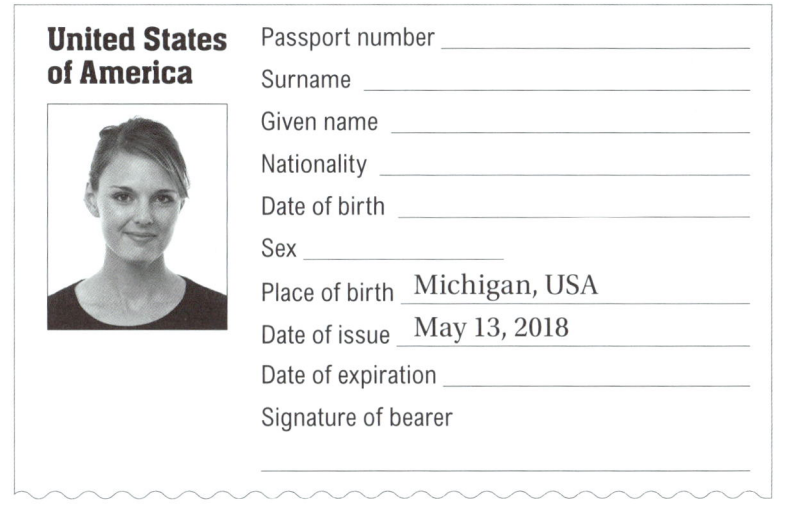

Jan 8, 1990
Smith
May 12, 2028
304407738
Lisa
Female
U.S.A.
Lisa Smith

United States of America

Passport number _____
Surname _____
Given name _____
Nationality _____
Date of birth _____
Sex _____
Place of birth Michigan, USA _____
Date of issue May 13, 2018 _____
Date of expiration _____
Signature of bearer
_____

(sidebar) Travel · Airline · Hotel

Listening 航空会社の案内係（男性）と乗客（女性）のダイアログを聞いてみましょう。   21

A Listen to the audio and check True or False.

1. Boarding will start in about 10 minutes. ☐ True ☐ False
2. The flight is on time. ☐ True ☐ False
3. The passenger's final destination is Montreal. ☐ True ☐ False

B Listen again and answer the following questions.

1. How long does the passenger have in Vancouver to catch the connecting flight?

   _____

2. What does the passenger need to do in Vancouver?

   _____

3. Who can board the airplane first?

   _____

今度はダイアログを読んで、その内容を確認しましょう。
次に音声を聞きながら練習をし、ペアで読み合わせをしましょう。

21

[At the gate]

Airline clerk: Ladies and gentlemen, Flight 201 will start boarding in another 10 minutes. **We apologize for** the **delay**.

Passenger: Excuse me. I have a **connecting flight** in Vancouver to go to Montreal. Do you think the delay will affect my connection?

Airline clerk: Let me see your ticket… You have two hours in Vancouver. That should allow you enough time to go through **immigration** and **customs**.

Passenger: Do I have to pick up my luggage?

Airline clerk: Yes. You need to go through customs with your baggage.

Passenger: Is Vancouver airport complicated?

Airline clerk: Well, it's not so complicated. Just follow the signs. After **customs inspection**, you will come to a **connection counter** where you can **drop off your luggage** for Montreal.

Passenger: OK.

Airline clerk: Oh, **it seems like** we can start boarding now. Have a nice flight. Ladies and gentlemen, thank you very much for waiting. Now we are ready to invite you on board. First class passengers, and passengers who have small children or who need assistance in boarding, please proceed to the gate now.

Vocabulary and Useful Expressions

We apologize for...	「…をお詫び申し上げます」 お客様には謝る機会が多いので覚えておきましょう。
delay	「遅延」 動詞も同じ形。 e.g. The flight is delayed due to the heavy snow.
connecting flight	「乗り継ぎ便」
immigration	「出入国管理」 go through immigration で「出入国手続きをする」という意味。
customs	「税関」 go through customs で「通関する」という意味。
customs inspection	「通関検査」
connection counter	「乗り継ぎ案内カウンター」 到着ロビーや、国によっては通関出口エリア付近にあります。
drop off your luggage	「荷物を乗り継ぎ便に載せるために渡す」 drop off は「荷物を降ろす」という意味。アメリカやカナダでは第一寄港地（the first port of entry）において入国検査が行われるため、乗り継ぐ場合は荷物をいったん引き取り、通関した後また預ける必要があります。
it seems like...	「…だと思われます」 明確でないときや自信がないときに使用しますが、断定しない言い方なので、ソフトな印象になります。

Travel

Airline

Hotel

Column

持ち主のいない荷物

お客様の搭乗が済んで、出発時刻も迫るころ、確認するとまだ1人の乗客が乗っていません。しばらく待ってもその乗客はやってきません。パイロットはどうすると思いますか。ほかのお客様の迷惑になるのでやむを得ずドアを閉めて飛び立つでしょうか。そのようなことは決してありません。地上要員は出発エリアを走り回り、必死にお客様を探します。なぜならば、チェックインした荷物だけが乗って本人が乗らないということは、その荷物が非常に危険なものである可能性があるからです。結局その乗客が見つからない場合は、ただちにその乗客の荷物を荷物室から降ろす作業が始まります。そのために、飛行機にはかなりの遅れが出てしまいます。搭乗時刻に遅れると、大迷惑になるということですね。

Pair Speaking Practice

以下の表現を使って会話練習をしましょう。

22

Airline clerk: **We apologize for** [1]the delay.

Passenger: [2]Why is it delayed?

Airline clerk: **It seems like** [3]there's some mechanical trouble.

Passenger: Oh, really? That's too bad.

	1	2	3
1st Time	the missing baggage	Do you know where it is?	it is still at Narita
2nd Time	the cancellation	What happened?	there's a typhoon approaching
3rd Time	the inconvenience	Why can't we get off the plane now?	the immigration area is crowded so we need to wait here

Role Play

ゲートでのお客様への対応を練習しましょう。
必要なセリフをダイアログから抜き出して覚え、交替でロールプレイをしてみましょう。

Student A

You are an airline clerk and work at a boarding gate. The next flight to Honolulu will be delayed 15 minutes. Make an announcement to let the passengers know. Answer the passenger's questions.

Student B

You are a passenger flying to Maui island via Honolulu. Your flight to Honolulu is delayed, so you are worried about your connecting flight to Maui. Show your ticket to the airline clerk and ask if there will be any connection problems.

Airline Ticket		
City	Departure/Arrival Time	Date
NRT – HNL	20:55 / 09:05	05 AUG 19
HNL – OGG	11:45 / 12:15	05 AUG 19

HNL = Honolulu Airport   OGG = Kahului Airport (Maui island)

Topic Reading **1** 空港のセキュリティーに関する注意書きを読んで、質問に答えましょう。

NOTICE | Airport security measures

In order to ensure flight safety, strict security measures are in force at passenger security screening checkpoints at this airport. Passengers' cooperation is appreciated.

For international flights, passengers may be asked to remove their shoes at the checkpoints. Coats and jackets must also be removed and scanned. Passengers may be asked to dispose of their liquid and/or gel items. Electronic items such as computers and tablets should be taken out of your bag and placed on the trays.

If knives, sharp instruments, scissors or other hazardous items are discovered at checkpoints, passengers will be asked to dispose of them. These items are strictly forbidden on board. Please make sure all such items are placed in your check-in luggage.

We understand that security screening can be inconvenient to passengers, but we ask for your patience and cooperation. Thank you very much.

Vocabulary Notes
■ measure「対策」 ■ in force「実施して」 ■ security screening「手荷物検査」
■ scan「(機械を通して) 検査をする」 ■ dispose of ...「...を廃棄する」

Q1 What are you expected to do at a security screening checkpoint at this airport?

a. Put your coat on
b. Take off your shoes
c. Keep your computer in your bag

Q2 If you want to pass through the checkpoint quickly, what should NOT you do?

a. Put your army knife in your check-in bag
b. Empty your drink bottle and dispose of it
c. Put your shampoo in your carry-on bag

Q3 If a pair of scissors is found in your carry-on bag at a security checkpoint, what do you have to do?

a. Ask an airline clerk to keep it until you arrive
b. Throw it away
c. Put it back in your carry-on bag

航空会社側の責任でフライトに大幅な遅れやキャンセルが生じた場合は、航空会社がそれに対して補償を行います。次のクーポン券を読んで、正誤問題に答えましょう。

Transportation credit voucher

☐ **$100 USD transportation credit or** ☐ **7,000 bonus miles**

This coupon is good for either $100 USD off the price of future travel on ABC Airlines or 7,000 bonus miles on your ABCFlyers account. Please indicate your choice above.

Customer name:

(please print)

Customer signature:

Travel must be completed within one year of the date of issue.

Date & place of issue:

Vocabulary Notes ▪ transportation「運賃」 ▪ credit voucher「引当金証書〔返金に相当する額を何らかの形で払うことを示した証書〕」

1. A passenger can use this $100 coupon when he/she takes a trip with the airline.   ☐ True   ☐ False

2. A passenger gets $100 credit plus 7,000 miles on his/her mileage account with this coupon.   ☐ True   ☐ False

3. A passenger can use this coupon anytime in the future.   ☐ True   ☐ False

4. A passenger needs to sign this coupon to use it.   ☐ True   ☐ False

Traveling Further

Airlines all over the world are trying hard to increase profits. Creating "alliances" is one strategy. Look for the names of airline alliances and find out which airlines belong to each alliance.

Unit 9

Offering in-flight services

一見華やかに見える客室乗務員 (flight attendant) ですが、その仕事は食事や飲み物のサービスだけにとどまらず、乳児連れの手助けから病人の介護などにも及びます。そして何よりも重要なのが、保安要員としての巡回や万が一の緊急時の救難作業であることはあまり知られていないかもしれません。

Travel

Airline

Hotel

Warm-up 救命胴衣 (life jacket) の使い方を前方スクリーンで説明しています。
英文を読みながら、絵を正しい順番に並べてみましょう。

"Your life jacket is located under your seat. Take it out from under your seat. Then pull the life jacket over your head. Fasten the jacket tightly with the straps around your waist. The jacket will inflate automatically after pulling the tags. If necessary, you can also inflate it by blowing into the tubes."

1. ☐ ▶ 2. ☐ ▶ 3. ☐ ▶ 4. ☐ ▶ 5. ☐

a	b	c	d	e
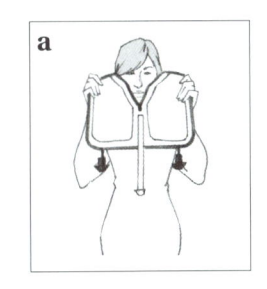	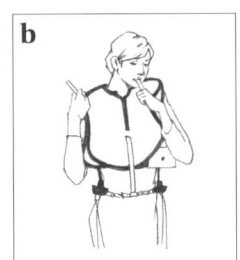	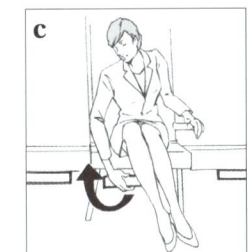	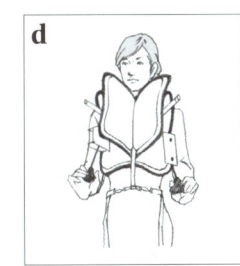	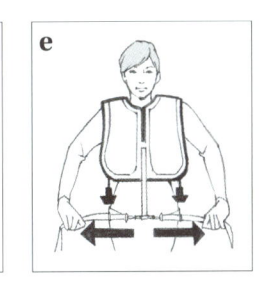

Listening 客室乗務員 (男性) と乗客 (主に女性) のダイアログを聞いてみましょう。

A Listen to the audio and check True or False.

[Scene 1] **1.** There is a passenger sitting in the wrong seat.　☐ True ☐ False

[Scene 2] **2.** The passenger will put the stroller under her seat.　☐ True ☐ False

[Scene 3] **3.** The passenger chose chicken for her meal.　☐ True ☐ False

B Listen again and answer the following questions.

[Scene 1] **1.** How many rows away is the passenger's actual seat?

_____

[Scene 2] **2.** Which lavatory has a diaper changing shelf?

_____

[Scene 3] **3.** What is the passenger drinking?

_____

[Scene 1: While boarding]

Flight attendant: **Welcome aboard.**

Passenger 1: Excuse me, it seems **someone is sitting in my seat**.

Flight attendant: Oh, may I see your boarding pass? *(Checking the boarding pass)* 45B. Let me check with the passenger. *(Talking to Passenger 2)* Excuse me, sir. May I see your boarding pass? *(Checking the boarding pass)* Thank you. Oh, this is 46B. I'm afraid your seat is the one right behind this.

Passenger 2: Oh, excuse me. Let me grab my things and move down.

[Scene 2: While boarding]

Passenger: Where can I put this stroller?

Flight attendant: We can keep it in the **stowage compartment**. I'll take care of it, ma'am.

Passenger: Thank you. Is there any place where I can change my baby's diaper?

Flight attendant: Yes, one of the **lavatories** in the back of the **cabin** has a **diaper changing shelf**.

Passenger: Good. Thank you.

Flight attendant: We have extra diapers and baby food **on board**. **Shall I** bring some for you**?**

Passenger: Well, I think I have everything, but I may need some baby food later.

Flight attendant: Please let me know at any time.

[Scene 3: During the meal service]

Flight attendant: **We have a choice of** chicken **or** beef. Which would you like?

Passenger: I would like the chicken, please.

Flight attendant: Here you are. **Would you care for** something to drink with it**?**

Passenger: Well, no thanks. I'm still working on my wine. I'll just have some coffee after the meal.

Flight attendant: All right, madam. We will come around with tea and coffee later.

Vocabulary and Useful Expressions

Welcome aboard.	「ようこそ」 飛行機や船舶でお客様を迎えるときの表現です。
someone is sitting in my seat	「私の席に座っている方がいます」 座席番号の間違いのほかに double booking といって、航空会社側のミスで同じ席が割り当てられてしまっていることもまれにあります。そうした場合は即座に地上係員と連絡を取り、違う席を割り当ててもらわなければなりません。
stowage compartment	「収納庫」 コート類をかけたり、座席下に収納できないものを入れたりする保管庫で、coat room と呼ぶこともあります。座席の上方にある荷物入れは overhead bin や overhead compartment などと呼びます。
lavatory	「お手洗い」
cabin	「客室」 これに対して cockpit は「操縦室」です。
diaper changing shelf	「オムツ交換用の台」 飛行機には1、2個所、この台が備わっているお手洗いがあります。
on board	「機内に」 on を使うことを覚えておきましょう。
Shall I...?	「…しましょうか」 申し出をするときに使用します。
We have a choice of A or B.	「A か B をお選びいただけます」
Would you care for...?	「…はいかがですか」= Would you like...?

Travel

Airline

Hotel

Column

緊急時の対応

フライトでは、離着陸時が全体の中で最も事故の可能性が高いと言われます。これを critical 11 minutes（危険な11分間）と呼び、離陸時の最初の3分と着陸時の8分間を合計したものです。客室乗務員は、離着陸時にはドアの横のジャンプシートに着席していますが、この時間帯には「今何かが起こったらどう対処すればよいか、何をどういう順番で行い、乗客には何と連呼すればよいか」ということを考えるように訓練されています。

Pair Speaking Practice

A お客様に申し出をする練習をしましょう。

Flight attendant: **Shall I** [1]take your coat**?**

Passenger: [2]Yes, please. Thank you.

	1	2
1st Time	bring you some water	No, I'm fine. Thank you.
2nd Time	put your bag in the stowage compartment	Yes. Thank you for your help.
3rd Time	help you carry your stroller	Thank you. It's very kind of you.

B 食事サービスの練習をしましょう。空欄は自分で考えて自由に埋めてみましょう。

Flight attendant: **Would you care for** something to drink**?**

Passenger: Yes, I would like some _____, please.

Flight attendant: Here you are. For lunch, **we have a choice of** _____ or _____. Which would you like/prefer?

Passenger: I'd like _____, please.

Role Play お客様の搭乗を迎えましょう。
必要なセリフをダイアログから抜き出して覚え、交替でロールプレイをしてみましょう。

Student A	Student B
You are a passenger flying with your baby. You have a stroller. You will probably need some powdered milk and diapers during the flight. You will need to change your baby's diaper, too.	You are a flight attendant. Try to help a mother/father with a baby. You can put the stroller in the stowage compartment. There are powdered milk, baby food and diapers on board. The lavatory with a changing shelf is on the left side in the back of the cabin.

機内アナウンスのスクリプトを読んで、正誤問題に答えましょう。

Welcome

Good afternoon, ladies and gentlemen. On behalf of Captain Yamaguchi and his crew, I would like to welcome you aboard ABC Airlines Flight 008 to Seattle. We are now ready for take-off, so you are requested to fasten your seatbelt at this time, and we recommend that you keep it fastened while seated. Our flight to Seattle will take 9 hours and 50 minutes. We wish you a pleasant flight. Thank you.

Arrival Information

Ladies and gentlemen, we will be landing at Seattle-Tacoma International Airport in about 30 minutes. The weather in Seattle is sunny and the temperature is 28°C. The local time is 3:35 in the afternoon. Transit passengers are required to go through immigration and customs at this airport. Please proceed to a transit desk after going through customs inspection. The captain has switched on the "seatbelt" sign. Please fasten your seatbelt, bring your seat to the fully upright position, and return your tray table to the original position. Thank you.

Vocabulary Notes ■ on behalf of...「…を代表して」 ■ transit「乗り継ぎ」

1. The welcome announcement was made by Captain Yamaguchi. ☐ True ☐ False

2. Passengers must have their seatbelts fastened at all times. ☐ True ☐ False

3. Upon arrival, transit passengers should proceed to their boarding gate at once. ☐ True ☐ False

4. In preparation for landing, passengers should put their tray tables back. ☐ True ☐ False

5. The weather at the destination is sunny. ☐ True ☐ False

Travel
Airline
Hotel

Your first-class experience starts with our priority check-in. Please enjoy a free pre-departure beverage in our First Class Lounge.

As soon as you enter the cabin, you will notice the difference. Our fully-enclosed seats offer you a private, comfortable space.

One of the highlights of our service is the choice of specially prepared meals. Our menu features a variety of options including local cuisine. All dishes are made-to-order fresh in our ovens and toasters. Enjoy our selection of quality champagne, international wines, cocktails, desserts and fruits. Snacks or light meals are available at any time during your flight. Ask any time for a cup of leaf tea or a freshly made cappuccino from our espresso machine.

After the pleasant feast, relax and enjoy our individual audio and video system. There are more than 20 featured films, 9 video channels and 21 music channels to choose from. Sit back and relax. The reclining angle of your seat is fully adjustable at the touch of a button, and our new seats can easily extend into a full-length bed.

Upon arrival, you will be among the first to leave the aircraft, and your bags among the first to be ready for collection.

Vocabulary Notes ■ enclosed「囲まれた」 ■ priority「優先」 ■ beverage「飲み物」
■ First Class Lounge「(空港内にある) ファーストクラス客専用ラウンジ」
■ made-to-order「注文を受けてから調理された」 ■ adjustable「調節可能な」

Q1 Before and after the flight, what privileges do first-class passengers have?

_____

Q2 How are dishes cooked in first class?

_____

Q3 What kinds of audio and video services are offered in first class?

_____

Q4 What kind of seats do they have in the first-class cabin?

_____

Traveling Further

Since Low Cost Carriers (LCC) started operating in the 1990s, the traditional airlines have been trying hard to compete against them. What LCCs are there in Japan or in other countries? Look for the names of LCCs and find out the characteristics of their services.

注：LCC = 低コスト航空会社

Giving CIQ information

CIQ とは Customs（通関）、Immigration（入国管理）、Quarantine（検疫）の頭文字をとったもので、海外から到着した旅客が通過する一連の手続きのことです。旅行代理店や航空会社では各国の CIQ に関する情報を旅客に提供することも重要な業務の一つです。

Warm-up　各写真の話している人物は誰でしょう？
customs officer、immigration officer、quarantine officer から選びましょう。

> Passport, please. What is the purpose of your visit?

> You need to get rid of these fruits and nuts. And you can't bring these dry flowers in. Sorry.

> Do you have anything to declare? Any liquor or cigarettes?

 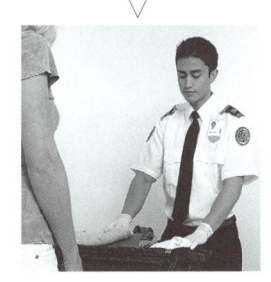 

1. [   ]　　2. [   ]　　3. [   ]

Travel　Airline　Hotel

Listening　機内での客室乗務員（女性）と乗客（男性）のダイアログを聞いてみましょう。 25

A　Listen to the audio and check True or False.

1. The passenger received two documents in total.　☐ True　☐ False
2. The passenger is traveling with his son.　☐ True　☐ False
3. The passenger will have to go through quarantine.　☐ True　☐ False

B　Listen again and answer the following questions.

1. What country is the passenger from?

_____

2. How many bottles of wine does the passenger have?

_____

3. Where does the passenger need to go after picking up his luggage?

_____

[During the flight]

Flight attendant: Do you have all the **necessary documents** to enter Australia?

Passenger: No, I don't think so. What do I need?

Flight attendant: **Are you a visitor** or an Australian**?**

Passenger: I am from Malaysia, visiting Australia on holiday.

Flight attendant: Then you will need an **entry form** when you go through immigration. You also need a **customs form**. Are you traveling alone?

Passenger: No, with my daughter.

Flight attendant: All right. Here are two entry cards and one customs form for you and your daughter. Only one customs form is needed per family. **Do you have anything to declare?**

Passenger: I'm not sure. I have six bottles of wine with me.

Flight attendant: The **duty-free allowance** for liquor into Australia is 2.25 liters per person, so you'll need to **make a customs declaration**. Please indicate the number of bottles on your customs form.

Passenger: All right. I also have some fresh fruit. Do I have to declare it?

Flight attendant: You need to go through **quarantine** for fruit. After you pick up your luggage at baggage claim, you should proceed to both the quarantine and customs counters.

Passenger: I see. Thank you very much.

Flight attendant: You're welcome. I hope you have a nice time in Australia.

Vocabulary and Useful Expressions

necessary documents
「必要書類」
外国に入国する場合は、入国カードや税関申告書などの書類が必要になります。飛行機の手配をした旅行代理店が航空券とともに旅客に渡すこともありますが、機内でも配布されます。

Are you a visitor?
「訪問者ですか」
多くの場合、訪問者 (visitors または non-residents) と国民 (citizens) で書類の種類や有無が異なります。

entry form/card
「入国書類／入国カード」
landing card や disembarkation card ともいいます。「出国カード」は embarkation card と呼ばれます。

customs form
「税関書類」

Do you have anything to declare?
「申告するものはありますか」
税関で聞かれる決まり文句です。

duty-free allowance
「免税範囲」
duty は tax と同じで「税」という意味です。国によって無税で持ち込めるお酒、タバコ、香水、ギフトなどの量が規定されており、この範囲を超える場合は税金がかかります。

make a customs declaration
「税関申告をする」= declare

quarantine
「検疫」
持ち込む動植物に関する検査で、入国者の病気のチェックもします。

Travel
Airline
Hotel

Column

オーストラリアの厳しい検疫

到着地の空港ではパスポートチェック (入国管理) と荷物チェック (税関) 以外に検疫検査を通過します。検疫の目的は当事国の動植物の天敵となる害虫や病原菌、また人にうつる感染症などが入らないようにすることです。通常は検査場を通り過ぎるだけですが、対象となる動植物を持っている場合、発熱や嘔吐などの症状がある場合は、立ち寄ってチェックを受けなくてはいけません。絶滅の危機に瀕している動物の多いオーストラリアでは特に検疫が厳しくて有名です。食品の持ち込みに関しても、フルーツや動物性の食物のみならず、様々な製品や加工品にまで細かい規制が及んでいます。

Pair Speaking Practice

お客様に免税に関する情報を提供しましょう。

26

Flight attendant: **Do you have anything to declare?**

Passenger: I'm not sure, but I have [1]six bottles of wine.

Flight attendant: **The duty-free allowance is** [2]two bottles, so you will have to **make a customs declaration**.

	1	2
1st Time	four bottles of perfume	three bottles
2nd Time	gifts worth 1,200 dollars each	100 dollars per gift
3rd Time	400 cigarettes	200 cigarettes

Role Play お客様に CIQ の情報を提供しましょう。
必要なセリフをダイアログから抜き出して覚え、交替でロールプレイをしてみましょう。

Student A

You are a flight attendant. Give a passenger immigration documents and necessary information. Look at your memo and answer the passenger's questions.

Student B

You are a Japanese student flying to Canada. Receive documents from a flight attendant and ask questions. You want to know if you need to make a customs declaration. You have a $100 (Canadian dollars) *yukata* that you will give as a gift. You also bought one carton of cigarettes on board. (One carton contains 200 cigarettes.)

MEMO

Immigration & customs information for Canada

<duty-free allowance>
wine: 1.5 L / beer: 8.5 L / other liquor: 1.14 L
200 cigarettes
gifts: $60 each (Canadian dollars)

<documents>
visitors: no entry form, one customs form per family

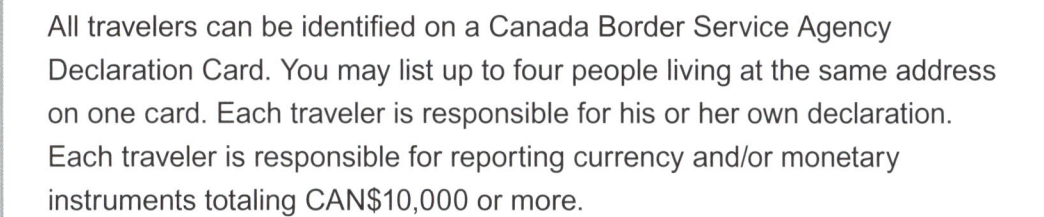

Topic Reading **1** カナダの税関申告書からの抜粋を読んで、正誤問題に答えましょう。

Part A All travelers

All travelers can be identified on a Canada Border Service Agency Declaration Card. You may list up to four people living at the same address on one card. Each traveler is responsible for his or her own declaration. Each traveler is responsible for reporting currency and/or monetary instruments totaling CAN$10,000 or more.

Part B Visitors to Canada

The following duty-free allowance applies to each visitor entering into Canada.
- Gifts (excludes alcohol and tobacco) valued at no more than CAN$60 each
- Alcohol and tobacco (see table)

Alcohol	Tobacco
1.5 L of wine or 1.14 L of liquor or 24 x 355 mL bottles/cans (8.5 L) of beer (You must be of legal age)	200 cigarettes, 200 tobacco sticks, 50 cigars and 200 g of manufactured tobacco (Special duty may apply)

Vocabulary Notes
- identify「身元を明らかにする〔この場合は名前を書き込むこと〕」
- Canada Border Service Agency「カナダ国境業務庁」
- monetary instruments「通貨代替物〔税関申告に関して、小切手などを指す〕」
- liquor「(蒸留)酒〔ウィスキーやウォッカなどのことで醸造酒と比べてアルコール度が高い〕」

Travel

Airline

Hotel

1. Family members need to live at the same address to use the same customs form. ☐ True ☐ False

2. Each person is responsible for reporting how much money they are bringing into Canada. ☐ True ☐ False

3. If a visitor to Canada has three gifts which are CAN$40 each, he/she doesn't have to pay duty. ☐ True ☐ False

4. Visitors to Canada can bring in 1.5 L of wine and one dozen 335 mL cans of beer without paying duty. ☐ True ☐ False

前のページで読んだ説明書を参照しながら、
お客様の情報を実際のカードに記入してみましょう。

Your Customer's Information

- Ms. Misaki is traveling to Canada with her daughter to visit a friend.
- Flight JL012 NRT—YVR (Vancouver)
- Ms. Misaki is flying on september 8, 2019.
- 〒162-0843 東京都新宿区市ヶ谷2-37
- 三咲 洋子 (みさき ようこ)
  1979年1月8日生まれ
- 三咲 理沙 (みさき りさ)
  2002年3月14日生まれ
- 滞在予定：7日
- 課税対象になるもの：CAN$100相当のお土産1つ
- 酒タバコ類、銃砲類、商品見本、動植物類などは所持せず。
- 別送品はなし。
- 農園に行く予定はなし。

I am/we are bringing into Canada:

- Firearms or other weapons
  (e.g. switchblades, mace or pepper spray).
- Commercial goods, whether or not for resale
  (e.g. samples, tools, equipment).
- Meat, fish, seafood, eggs, dairy products, fruits, vegetables, seeds, nuts, plants, flowers, wood, animals, birds, insects, and any parts, products or by-products of any of the foregoing.
- Currency and/or monetary instruments totaling CAN$10,000 or more.

I/we have unaccompanied goods.

I/we have visited a farm and will be going to a farm in Canada.

Declaration Card (Canada Border Services Agency / Agence des services frontaliers du Canada)

— For Agency Use Only —
PAX   R   U.S. V   OV   Cr   O

Part A | All travellers (living at the same address) -- Please print in capital letters.

1. Last name, first name and initials — Date of birth: YY - MM - DD — Citizenship:
2. Last name, first name and initials — Date of birth: YY - MM - DD — Citizenship:
3. Last name, first name and initials — Date of birth: YY - MM - DD — Citizenship:
4. Last name, first name and initials — Date of birth: YY - MM - DD — Citizenship:

HOME ADDRESS – Number, street, apartment No. | City/Town

Prov./State | Country | Postal/Zip code

Arriving by: Air / Rail / Marine / Highway
Airline/flight No., train No. or vessel name

Purpose of trip: Study / Personal / Business

Arriving from: U.S. only / Other country direct / Other country via U.S.

I am/we are bringing into Canada: | Yes | No
- Firearms or other weapons (e.g. switchblades, Mace or pepper spray).
- Commercial goods, whether or not for resale (e.g. samples, tools, equipment).
- Meat, fish, seafood, eggs, dairy products, fruits, vegetables, seeds, nuts, plants, flowers, wood, animals, birds, insects, and any parts, products or by-products of any of the foregoing.
- Currency and/or monetary instruments totaling CAN$10,000 or more.

I/we have unaccompanied goods.

I/we have visited a farm and will be going to a farm in Canada.

Part B | Visitors to Canada
Duration of stay in Canada ___ days | Do you or any person listed above exceed the duty-free allowances per person? (See instructions on the left.) | Yes | No

Part C | Residents of Canada
Do you or any person listed above exceed the exemptions per person? (See instructions on the left.) | Yes | No

Complete in the same order as Part A

	Date left Canada YY - MM - DD	Value of goods – CAN$ purchased or received abroad (including gifts, alcohol & tobacco)		Date left Canada YY - MM - DD	Value of goods – CAN$ purchased or received abroad (including gifts, alcohol & tobacco)
1			3		
2			4		

Part D | Signatures (age 16 and older): I certify that my declaration is true and complete.
1
2   Date YY - MM - DD
3
4

E311 (16)   Protected A when completed
Do not fold Declaration Card
Canada

Vocabulary Notes
- citizenship「市民権〔書類では市民権のある国名を記入。nationality と表記しているカードも多い〕」   - firearm「銃」
- unaccompanied goods「別送品〔ここでは携帯せずにカナダへ送っている物品のことを指す〕」

Taking a room reservation

ホテルには様々な電話がかかってきます。宿泊客を呼び出す電話、予約の電話、問い合わせの電話などです。ここでは宿泊を検討しているお客様からの問い合わせの電話を取ってみましょう。

Warm-up

宿泊施設には料金や用途によって様々なタイプがあります。
以下の代表的な宿泊施設の例（1–6）とそのキーワード（a–f）をつないでみましょう。

1. Hostel

2. Motel

3. Hotel

4. Bed & Breakfast (B&B)

5. Boutique hotel

6. Resort hotel

a. Inexpensive usually with shared bedrooms and communal facilities

b. Small, designer furnishings, fashionable

c. Independently run, breakfast included

d. Vacations, variety of facilities, relaxation

e. Many guest rooms, common reception area, restaurants open to public

f. Roadside, large parking lot

Travel
Airline
Hotel

Listening

ホテルの予約担当者（男性）とお客様（女性）のダイアログを聞いてみましょう。

 27

A Listen to the audio and check True or False.

1. The breakfast is included in the room rate. ☐ True ☐ False
2. The hotel doesn't have a fitness room. ☐ True ☐ False
3. A gift certificate is given to guests staying this Sunday. ☐ True ☐ False

B Listen again and answer the following questions.

1. What is their rate for a double room?

_____

2. Where can guests use the gift certificate?

_____

3. What kind of room did the guest reserve?

_____

[At the hotel back office]

Caller: Hi. I'd like to find out your **rate** for a **single room** this coming weekend.

Reservation clerk: Single rooms are 10,500 yen per night, with breakfast.

Caller: Does that include tax and **service charges**?

Reservation clerk: **Service charges are included in the rate**, but not the tax.

Caller: I see. How about a **double room**?

Reservation clerk: Double rooms are 18,000 yen per night, with breakfast.

Caller: All right. Do you still have a single room available this weekend?

Reservation clerk: For one night?

Caller: No, two nights. Friday and Saturday.

Reservation clerk: One moment, madam. I'll check for you… Yes, **we have a single room available on both nights**. We are now **running a promotion** for those guests who are staying with us more than two nights. We are **giving away** a 2,000-yen **gift certificate** to use at any of our hotel restaurants, bars or beauty salons.

Caller: Oh, that sounds good. Does your hotel have any sports **facilities**?

Reservation clerk: Yes. We have a fitness room and a heated swimming pool available to all our guests.

Caller: That's good. Are you close to a train station?

Reservation clerk: Yes, there is a subway station just a one-minute walk away.

Caller: OK, I'd like to reserve a single room.

Reservation clerk: All right, madam. So, you are checking in on the 20th and checking out on the 22nd?

Caller: Yes, that's right…

Vocabulary and Useful Expressions

rate	「料金」 room rate は「客室料金」。room charge ともいいます。
single room	「シングルルーム」
service charge	「サービス料」 ホテルや高級レストランなどでチップの代わりに料金に上乗せするもの。10〜15% が相場ですが、不透明感があるため、廃止するホテルや、料金に含めて価格表示するホテルも増えています。
Service charges are included in the rate.	「料金はサービス料込みです」 〈A is included in B〉の表現を覚えましょう。
double room	「ダブルベッドがある2人用の部屋」 twin room: 2つのシングルベッドがある2人用の部屋 connecting room: 2つの部屋が室内のドアでつながっているタイプの部屋で、家族連れやグループなどに便利 suite: スイートルーム。寝室のほかにリビングルームなどもある豪華な特別室
we have a single room available on both nights	「両日ともシングルルームの空きがあります」 we have A (room type) available on B (date/day) の文で覚えましょう。
run a promotion	「キャンペーンを行う」
give away	「プレゼントする」 giveaway で「景品」という意味。
gift certificate	「ギフト券、商品券」
facility	「設備」 ホテルの設備に加え、快適さを追求するためのサービス項目も含めて amenity (amenities) または feature(s) と表現することもあります。free parking、high-speed Internet access、newspaper、business center、pets allowed、laundry、gift shop、safe-deposit box、multilingual staff などがその例です。

Travel　Airline　Hotel

Column

おもてなしの心

「サービス」と「ホスピタリティ」の違いとは何でしょうか？ service の語源は servus で「奴隷」という意味です。ですから、その概念は義務的に相手に奉仕するというものになります。hospitality の語源はラテン語の hospitalis で、「相手を厚遇する」という意味です。すなわちその概念は、相手を喜ばそう、満足させてあげようという気持ちです。この語源から派生したのが hotel や hospital などです。ホスピタリティは相手の置かれた状況を判断し、義務やマニュアルにとらわれない心からのおもてなしを提供するということだと言えるでしょう。

Pair Speaking Practice

ホテルへの問い合わせに対し、室料と空室状況を教える練習をしましょう。

28

Caller: I'd like to find out your rate for a [1]single room.

Reservation clerk: [1]Single rooms are [2]$100 per night. [3]**The service charge is included** in the rate.

Caller: I see. Do you have a [1]single room available [4]on June 30?

Reservation clerk: Yes, **we have a** [1]**single room available on that day.**

(No, I'm afraid we have no [1]single rooms available on that day.)

	1	2	3	4
1st Time	single	$85	Breakfast is included.	this weekend
2nd Time	double	¥18,000	The service charge and tax are included.	on May 4
3rd Time	suite	$560	The service charge and tax are not included.	on Christmas Eve

Role Play 問い合わせに対応しましょう。
必要なセリフをダイアログから抜き出して覚え、交替でロールプレイをしてみましょう。

Student A

You are planning a trip. Decide when you want to stay at a hotel and what type of a room you want. Then call a hotel and ask about the availability and rate.

Student B

You are a hotel reservation clerk. Look at the calendar. All the weekends (Friday through Sunday) are fully booked this month, but all kinds of rooms are still available Monday through Thursday. Your hotel's rates with breakfast: single, ¥8,000; double, ¥16,000; twin, ¥17,000; suite, ¥49,000. Service charges and tax are not included.

March						
Mo	**Tu**	**We**	**Th**	**Fr**	**Sa**	**Su**
			1	2	3	4
5	6	7	8	9	10	11
12	13	14	15	16	17	18
19	20	21	22	23	24	25
26	27	28	29	30	31	

Room Type: single, double, twin, suite

Topic Reading　1　ホテルの会員 (membership) プログラムの宣伝を読んで、正誤問題に答えましょう。

Get More from Every Stay!!

Enjoystay Club Rewards is the travel rewards program that makes it easier to earn, easier to redeem, easier to enjoy rewards.
Program benefits include:

- Over 500 locations at which to earn and redeem points
- No blackout dates
- Points transferable between accounts of family members
- Points never expire
- Fastest way to Gold status
- At any of our affiliated hotels, anytime, anywhere

Point redemption: This program allows members to redeem their points for free stays at over 500 lodging establishments worldwide.

For more details on member benefits, to check your point balance or to learn more about ways to earn more points, visit **enjoystay.com**.

Vocabulary Notes
- rewards program「特典プログラム」　■ blackout dates「利用不可の日〔たいてい繁忙期に設定される〕」
- accounts「(ポイントの) 口座」　■ expire「有効期限切れになる」
- Gold status「ゴールドメンバー〔ポイントがたまるとランクアップしていくシステム〕」　■ affiliated「提携の」
- redemption「(ポイントの) 交換〔動詞 redeem の名詞形〕」

1. Members can use their points to stay at affiliated hotels, except during the holiday season.　☐ True　☐ False

2. Club members must use their points within three years.　☐ True　☐ False

3. Family members can share points for redemption.　☐ True　☐ False

4. Your point status can be checked online.　☐ True　☐ False

An Unusual Hotel

There are a lot of unique or unusual hotels in the world. One such hotel is a cave hotel near Granada, Spain. It is a prehistoric cave habitation, now converted into individual cottages for year-round guest accommodation. With all rooms featuring modern living facilities, Caves Pedro Antonio de Alarcón Hotel offers high-quality service.

Inside the complex of 23 caves, the temperature is kept at 19 degrees. The caves are located in a clay hillside. From the outside, the white fireplace chimneys dotting this hillside are the only indication that the hotel exists. Every cave has a fully-equipped kitchen, a living room with TV and telephone, bedrooms and bathrooms. Rooms are equipped with central heating and ventilation.

The complex also houses a laundry, a meeting room, an outdoor swimming pool and a restaurant where you can taste traditional Granadian dishes. Room service and an activity booking service are also available. The hotel is located about 60 km from Granada Airport.

Vocabulary Notes　■ Granada「グラナダ〔スペイン南部の都市〕」　■ prehistoric「有史以前の」　■ habitation「住居」　■ complex「複合施設」　■ fully-equipped「完全装備の」　■ ventilation「空調」　■ Granadian「グラナダ風の」

Q1 What is unique about this hotel?

Q2 What can be seen of this hotel from the outside?

Q3 What are the cottages like?

Q4 How far is this hotel from the nearest airport?

Traveling Further

Search for an interesting, unusual or unique hotel. Where is it? Why is it unique? Share your findings with your classmates.

Unit
12
Welcoming guests

ホテルのフロントはまさしくホテルの顔と言ってもよいでしょう。到着したお客様に応じて、優雅で迅速、そして機転の利くサービスが求められます。

Warm-up ホテルに到着したお客様はどのような気持ちでいるでしょうか。
そのときの気持ちを想像し、それぞれのお客様に対してどのように接したらよいかを考えて、
枠内のキーワードを参考にしながら表を作成してみましょう。

Guest(s)	Situation	Feelings	How do you treat/speak to them?
family	vacation	happy & cheerful	with a friendly smile
businessman	business		
honeymooners	honeymoon		
elderly couple	relative's wedding		
student alone	taking college exam		

Keywords	**Feelings:** nervous, shy, busy, tired, romantic, uncertain, curious, stressed **How do you treat/speak to them:** kind manner, caring manner, friendly manner, slowly, politely, quickly, without interrupting, respectfully, efficiently

Listening ホテルのフロント係（女性）と到着したお客様（男性）のダイアログを聞いてみましょう。

A Listen to the audio and check True or False.

1. The guest will stay at the hotel for three nights. ☐ True ☐ False
2. Breakfast is served between 6 a.m. and 10 a.m. ☐ True ☐ False
3. The guest asked the porter for help with his luggage. ☐ True ☐ False

B Listen again and answer the following questions.

1. When is the guest going to check out of the hotel? _____

2. What two things did the front desk clerk ask the guest to do?

_____

3. Where is the elevator?

_____

[At the front desk]

Front desk clerk: Good evening, sir. Are you checking in?

Guest: Yes, I have a reservation for two nights. My name is Robert Baum.

Front desk clerk: Yes, Mr. Baum. Let me see..., a non-smoking single room for two nights, checking out on the 8th.

Guest: That's right.

Front desk clerk: **Will you** fill out this **registration form** and sign at the bottom**, please?**

Guest: Sure. *(Filling out the form)* Here you are.

Front desk clerk: Thank you, Mr. Baum. **Could I have your credit card?**

Guest: All right. Here you are.

Front desk clerk: Thank you, sir. Just a moment, please... Here is your credit card back. This is your **key card**. Your room is 912, on the 9th floor.

Guest: OK. Thank you.

Front desk clerk: Here are breakfast **coupons** for both mornings. **Breakfast is served at** the Sunrise Café **on** the second floor, **from** 6:00 a.m. **to** 10:00 a.m. Just present your coupon at the restaurant entrance.

Guest: Great. Which way is the elevator?

Front desk clerk: It is over there at the end of the hall. Would you like a **porter** to help you with your luggage?

Guest: No, thank you. I can handle it.

Front desk clerk: All right. Enjoy your stay, Mr. Baum.

Vocabulary and Useful Expressions

Will you…, please?	「…していただけますか」 依頼をする際の丁寧な言い方。Would you や Could you と同じ。
registration form	「宿泊カード」 guest information form とも呼ばれ、名前、住所、連絡先などをチェックイン時に記入してもらいます。
Could I have your credit card?	「クレジットカードを確認させていただいてよろしいですか」 Could I...? は丁寧に許可を尋ねる言い方。宿泊料の不払いを防ぐために、このダイアログのようにチェックイン時にクレジットカード番号をあらかじめ控えておくホテルがあります〔欧米系ホテルに多い〕。また、no-show（キャンセルの連絡なし）や無責任な予約を防止するために、予約時にカード番号を控える（card guarantee）システムを採用しているホテルもあります。さらに、予約から一定の期限内に予約金を入金するよう求めるホテルもあります。その一方で、そのようなことは一切せず、すべてお客様とホテルとの信頼をベースに経営しているホテルもあります。
key card	「カードキー」 セキュリティ上、通常の金属製のカギではなく、宿泊者が変わるごとにデータを入れ替えられるタイプのカード式が主流になっています。
coupon	「クーポン券」= voucher
Breakfast is served at A on B floor, from C to D.	「朝食は B 階にある A にて、C 時から D 時までお召し上がりいただけます」 定型文として覚えておきましょう。
porter	「ポーター」 空港やホテルで荷物の運搬を手伝うスタッフ。アメリカでは bellboy と呼ぶほうが一般的で、主にホテルで使用される職名です。「ボーイ長」は bell captain といいます。

Travel
Airline
Hotel

Column

ホテルの格付け

ホテルの格付けは、有力な雑誌や民間調査機関などが行っており、世界的な統一基準があるわけではありません。雑誌で有名なのは『ミシュランガイド』や『ザガットサーベイ』、『フォーブス・トラベルガイド』などで、定期的にランク付けのための調査を行っています。例えば『フォーブス・トラベルガイド』では900にも及ぶ項目の覆面調査を行って5つ星〜4つ星レベルのホテルやレストランを選び、毎年発表しています。

Pair Speaking Practice

A Could I...? を使ってパートナーに3つの事項を依頼してみましょう。その際にパートナーの反応をメモしましょう。

A: **Could I** [1]see your ID card**?**

B: [2]Sure. / All right. / OK. / No problem. / I'm sorry, but... / No, I'm afraid...

	1	2
1st Time		
2nd Time		
3rd Time		

B お客様に以下の案内をしましょう。　　　　　　　　　　　　　　　　　　　🎧 30

Guest: Where is [1]breakfast served?

Front desk clerk: [1]**Breakfast is served at the** [2]**Sunrise Café on the** [3]**second floor, from** [4]**6:00 a.m. to 10:00 a.m.** Just present your [5]coupon at the restaurant entrance.

	1	2	3	4	5
1st Time	lunch	Holiday Restaurant	3rd floor	11:30 a.m. to 2:30 p.m.	coupon
2nd Time	dinner	Sky Grill	15th floor	5:30 p.m. to 10:00 p.m.	voucher
3rd Time	a welcome cocktail	Star Lounge	16th floor	7:00 p.m.	welcome drink ticket

Role Play　チェックインのお客様に対応しましょう。
必要なセリフをダイアログから抜き出して覚え、交替でロールプレイをしてみましょう。

Student A

You are a hotel guest. You reserved a non-smoking single room for three nights.

Student B

You are a front desk clerk. Welcome your guest and check him/her in. Make sure to ask your guest to fill in the registration form. Give him/her a key and breakfast coupons. The guest's room is 412, on the 4th floor.

Reservation Record

Name	Mr./Ms. *your partner's name*
Date	In: Aug 9　　Out: Aug 12
Rm Type	Single Rm (Non-smoking)

Topic Reading 1

宿泊予約の規約を読んで、正誤問題に答えましょう。

Rainbow Hotel Room Reservation Terms & Conditions

- Deposit—Your credit card will be charged immediately for the first night's room rate plus tax. Special packages may require full prepayment.

- All room rates are subject to a 8.0% tax.

- All reservation requests must include the first and last name of the adult occupying the room.

- The charge for additional occupants is $35 per person per night. Maximum occupancy is four persons per room.

- Bed type, smoking/non-smoking preference and other requests are noted but are NOT GUARANTEED, and will be honored on a space-available basis.

- There is a 48-HOUR CANCELLATION POLICY. Deposits are refundable upon notice of cancellation by midnight, 48 hours prior to your arrival date. No refunds will be made without a valid cancellation number.

- Internet rates are not valid in conjunction with other discount programs.

- Check-in time is 3:00 p.m. and check-out time is 12:00 p.m.

- For changes or cancellations, please call 1-800-732-7117.

Vocabulary Notes
- terms and conditions「契約条件」 - deposit「前金」 - be subject to tax「課税対象である」
- occupancy「収容定員」 - on a space-available basis「空室状況に基づいて」
- refundable「返金可能で」 - in conjunction with...「…と併用して」

---

1. You must pay for the first night at the time of your reservation. ☐ True ☐ False

2. Extra guests can stay in the same room without any extra charge. ☐ True ☐ False

3. Requests for room types are always granted. ☐ True ☐ False

4. If you cancel a day before, you will get your deposit back. ☐ True ☐ False

5. If you don't have a cancellation number, there will be no refund. ☐ True ☐ False

6. Internet rates can be combined with other discount programs. ☐ True ☐ False

LAS VEGAS DOLPHIN HOTEL

Our Hotel: Set against a panoramic desert skyline, the Las Vegas Dolphin Hotel in Las Vegas, Nevada, is just two blocks from the famed Las Vegas Strip and immediately adjacent to the Las Vegas Convention Center. Our hotel ranks among the world's most famous and popular resort destinations, and each year provides two million guests with the highest standard of service.

Hotel Amenities: Swimming pool, whirlpool jacuzzi, tennis courts, fitness gym, wheelchair-accessible rooms, luggage service, room service, in-room Internet access, concierge, safety deposit boxes, currency exchange.

Guest Accommodations: Standard rooms are decorated in a warm contemporary style. Every room offers an extraordinary view of the Las Vegas Strip, the mountains, or the nearby golf course.

Vocabulary Notes
- Las Vegas Strip「派手な建築のホテルが立ち並ぶラスベガスの目抜き通り」 ■ adjacent to...「…に隣接した」
- convention center「コンベンションセンター〔会議や展示会を目的として建設された国際大会議場〕」
- whirlpool jacuzzi「泡風呂」 ■ accommodations「宿泊設備」

Q1 What sports facilities does this hotel offer?

_____

Q2 What are the guest rooms like?

_____

Q3 What do you think are the selling points of this hotel? Write your own ideas.

_____

Traveling Further

Find websites of one resort hotel and one city hotel. Then compare the types of rooms, rates, and facilities or amenities. Report your findings in class.

Helping guests

コンシェルジュ (concierge) とは宿泊客のプライベートな相談に応じ、より快適で楽しい滞在ができるよう手助けする役目を担います。主に観光や食事に関する情報を提供したり、買い物のアドバイスや各種予約の手伝いを行ったりします。

Warm-up

ホテルには様々な職種があります。仕事内容 (1–6) にあてはまる職名 (a–f) を枠内から選び、□に記入しましょう。

a. front desk clerk	**b.** reservation clerk
c. doorman	**d.** housekeeper
e. bell captain	**f.** concierge

I take care of guests' luggage.

I welcome guests at the entrance.

I clean the guests' rooms.

I book the rooms for customers.

I try to help guests in any way possible.

I check guests in and out.

1. □ **2.** □ **3.** □ **4.** □ **5.** □ **6.** □

Travel · Airline · Hotel

Listening ホテルのコンシェルジュ (男性) と宿泊客 (女性) のダイアログを聞いてみましょう。 🎧 31

A Listen to the audio and check True or False.

1. The tour costs 4,600 yen. □ True □ False
2. The tour bus will come to the hotel at 8:30. □ True □ False
3. Tokyo Station is five stops away from the hotel. □ True □ False

B Listen again and answer the following questions.

1. Which sightseeing spots does the tour cover?

   _____

2. Did the guest choose the tour? Why or why not?

   _____

3. When does the guest want to go to Nikko?

   _____

[At the concierge desk]

Guest: Excuse me. I would like to take a day trip to Nikko. Can you help me plan the day?

Concierge: Certainly, madam. There are two options. One option is to join a bus tour with an English-speaking guide. The tour includes a Japanese-style lunch. Another option is to use the **express train** to get there and explore the area by yourself.

Guest: Oh, there is a bus tour. How much does it cost?

Concierge: It is 5,600 yen per adult.

Guest: Not bad. Which **sightseeing spots** does the tour cover?

Concierge: Most of the main **sights** and **attractions** in the area. Here is a brochure, if you are interested. The tour bus will stop in front of this hotel at 8:30 to **pick up** tour members.

Guest: That sounds very convenient. Now, how do I get to Nikko by myself?

Concierge: First, **take the subway to Tokyo Station**. The subway station across the street from here is only **one stop away from** Tokyo Station. Then **change trains** to the Tohoku Shinkansen Line. At Utsunomiya, change trains to the JR Nikko Line.

Guest: Well, I think I'll just join the bus tour. It is probably more convenient.

Concierge: Good choice, madam. When would you like to go?

Guest: Tomorrow. I have a day off from work.

Concierge: Oh, you're here **on business**. It's nice that you have some time to enjoy sightseeing. **Would you like me to** call the company to book the tour for you**?**

Guest: Yes, please.

Concierge: May I have your name and room number, please?

Guest: It's Martin, Jane Martin, in Room 809.

Concierge: OK, Ms. Martin, let me call the tour company now. Just a second, please.

Vocabulary and Useful Expressions

express train	「急行列車」 「新幹線」は bullet train と呼ぶこともありますが、多くの場合 Shinkansen とそのまま表現されます。なお、「普通列車、各駅停車」は local train です。
sightseeing spot	「観光地、見どころ」
sight(s)	「名所」
attraction(s)	「呼び物」
pick up	「(車やバスで) 迎える」 e.g. Our tour guide will pick you up at the airport.
take the subway to Tokyo Station	「東京駅まで地下鉄を利用する」 行き方を教える表現です。take A (乗り物) to B (場所) という構文で覚えましょう。「…行きの列車」は train bound for (場所) で表します。
one stop (away) from…	「…から1つめの駅」 駅やバス停がいくつめかを数えるときに stop で表現します。
change trains	「(列車を) 乗り換える」 change trains at (場所) to the A Line のように前置詞を使います。
on business	「出張で」 「出張客」は business traveler です。
Would you like me to…?	「…いたしましょうか」 Do you want to me to…? の丁寧な言い方です。Shall I…? と同じ意味になります。

Travel

Airline

Hotel

Column

接客の専門職

コンシェルジュ (concierge) とは、もともとフランスの高級アパートにいる住み込み管理人のことで、住人が快適に暮らせるように守衛の役目のほか、さまざまな世話や雑用を行っていました。やがて、ホテル業界でコンシェルジュという役職がサービスの質の良さを表すものとして重要視されるようになりました。今でも限られたホテルにしか置かれていませんが、多くのコンシェルジュは、宿泊客からのあらゆる要望に応じるということをモットーとしています。

Pair Speaking Practice

A 路線図の中から駅を1つ選び（下線部1）、行き方を尋ねてみましょう（下線部2〜4/5）。
尋ねられた人は、行き方を説明しましょう。 🎧 32

> Guest: How can I get to [1]Tsukuba?
>
> Concierge: **Take the [2]Yamanote Line to [3]Akihabara. It is [4]three stops away from here.**
>
> (Then, change trains to the [5]Tsukuba Express Line.)

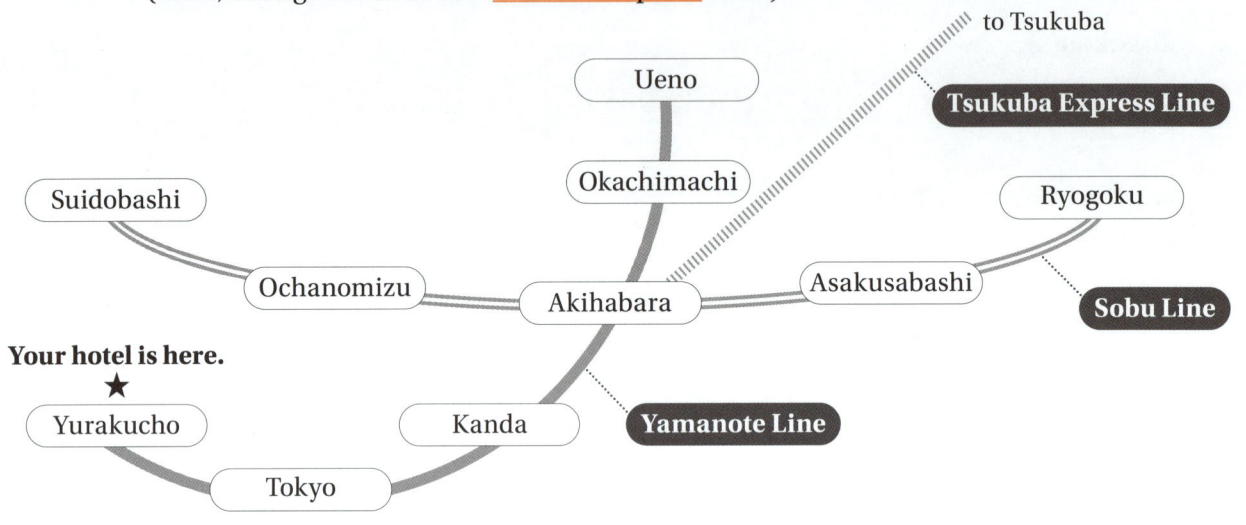

B お客様に丁寧に提案をしてみましょう。 🎧 33

> Concierge: **Would you like me to call the company?**
>
> Guest: Yes, thank you. / No, that's OK.

1st Time	draw you a map	3rd Time	post this letter for you
2nd Time	call a porter	4th Time	*think of your own*

Role Play お客様のリクエストに答えましょう。
必要なセリフをダイアログから抜き出して覚え、交替でロールプレイをしてみましょう。

Student A	Student B
You are a hotel guest in Osaka. You have a day off from work tomorrow and want to visit Kyoto. Ask for information.	You are a concierge. Your hotel guest would like to take a day trip to Kyoto. Tell him/her how to get there from your hotel in Osaka. Also recommend a bus tour.

[Option 1] Getting to Kyoto by him-/herself

by the JR Tokaido Line, two stops on the express train (30 minutes)

[Option 2] A full-day bus tour to Kyoto

Departure: 9:00 a.m. from Osaka Station bus terminal

Return: 5:00 p.m. with English-speaking guide & Japanese lunch

Fee: adult 6,000 yen / child (up to 12 years old) 3,000 yen

Topic Reading **1** Mr. Lee がチェックイン時に受け取った手紙を読んで、質問に答えましょう。

CARLTON HOTEL TOKYO

Dear Mr. Lee,

A warm welcome on your return to Carlton Hotel Tokyo! We are delighted that you have chosen to stay with us once again, and we hope you will continue to find that our facilities and personalized service meet your every need.

It is our pleasure to invite you to visit our exclusive Executive Floor Lounge on the 25th floor, which is open from 6 a.m. until 11 p.m. daily. The Executive Floor Lounge offers refined service to meet all your business and leisure requirements: a convenient meeting room, express laundry service, dining facilities including buffet breakfast, afternoon tea and evening cocktails. While staying with us, you are also welcome to invite your guests to the Executive Floor Lounge, where there will only be a charge for their drinks and food.

If there is anything else that we can do to make your stay more pleasant, please contact us directly using the one-touch Guest Hotline button on your telephone.

Yours sincerely,

Minami Ouchi

(Ms.) Minami Ouchi
Assistant Executive Floor Manager

Vocabulary Notes
- personalized service「個々に対応したサービス」 ▪ exclusive「専用の」
- executive floor「エグゼクティブ・フロア〔企業の上級管理職層を対象にしたフロアで部屋のグレードアップのほか、専用ラウンジなどが用意されている〕」 ▪ refined service「きめ細やかなサービス」

Travel

Airline

Hotel

Q1 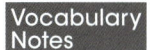 **What is this letter mainly about?**

   a. A promotion of new gift shops

   b. An invitation to the hotel

   c. An introduction to the Executive Floor Lounge

Q2 **Which of the following is probably true about Mr. Lee?**

   a. He is a first-time guest at this hotel.

   b. He has stayed at this hotel at least once before.

   c. He has visited this hotel several times.

Q3 **What can you do in the Executive Floor Lounge?**

   a. Bring your guests for a discount lounge fee

   b. Invite your friends to eat and drink at no charge

   c. Use facilities for meetings or dining

Experience Omotenashi   Japanese style hospitality

If you are planning to visit Japan, consider staying at a ryokan. Ryokans are Japanese-style inns that are typically found in areas with hot springs. They provide an atmosphere of Japanese "wa" (harmony) and often serve as a symbol of Japanese omotenashi. Omotenashi is the leading principle of most ryokans. From welcoming the guests to bidding them farewell, staff at ryokans not only put guests first but also pay attention to every detail to ensure their satisfaction.

It is believed that the omotenashi spirit has its roots in the traditional tea ceremony (chanoyu) where tea masters face their guests and make tea in front of them. The purpose of the tea ceremony is not just to drink tea, but rather to have a special moment with the guests. Omotenashi, therefore, is not only about manners, but it is also about exceeding expectations and anticipating the needs of guests.

With increasing numbers of inbound tourists, Japanese ryokans aim to improve their omotenashi, and thereby create even better opportunities for international tourists to experience genuine Japanese "wa" culture and omotenashi.

Vocabulary Notes
- principle「行動規範」
- bid farewell「お別れする」
- exceed expectations「期待を超える」
- anticipate the needs of...「…のニーズを察知する」
- genuine「真の」

Q1 What are some features of ryokan?

_____

Q2 Describe the characteristics of omotenashi.

_____

Q3 What kind of improvements do you think ryokans can make for international visitors? Write down your ideas.

_____

Traveling Further

The job of a concierge is an example of giving excellent service to customers. Visit the Les Clefs d'Or website at www.lesclefsdor.org (English version) and find out more about a concierge's work.

Dealing with complaints

ホテルに滞在中のお客様からは様々な要望、問題、苦情が寄せられます。対処の仕方は状況に応じて変わります。特に苦情処理は対応に苦労することもありますが、お客様が納得できる解決策を提供できるよう私情を交えず、迅速に真摯な態度で取り組むことが大事です。

Warm-up

ホテルにはどのような要望(requests)、問題(problems)、苦情(complaints) が寄せられるでしょうか。グループで考えてみましょう。意見が出たら、自分たちならどのように対処するか考えてみましょう。そして、他のグループと結果をシェアしましょう。

	What is your guess?	How do you deal with it?
Requests		
Problems		
Complaints		

Listening

ホテルのフロント係 (女性) と宿泊客 (男性) のダイアログを聞いてみましょう。 34

A Listen to the audio and check True or False.

[Scene 1] **1.** Mr. Chen has a problem with the shower in his room. ☐ True ☐ False

[Scene 2] **2.** Mr. Rex checked into a room with a city view. ☐ True ☐ False

3. The front desk clerk asked Mr. Rex to wait in the lobby. ☐ True ☐ False

B Listen again and answer the following questions.

[Scene 1] **1.** How did the front desk clerk deal with Mr. Chen's problem?

_____

[Scene 2] **2.** What was Mr. Rex's request?

_____

3. How did the front desk clerk deal with Mr. Rex's request?

_____

Travel ✕ Airline 🏨 Hotel

Dialogue Study 今度はダイアログを読んで、その内容を確認しましょう。
次に音声を聞きながら練習をし、ペアで読み合わせをしましょう。

[Scene 1: At a hotel]

Front desk clerk: Hello, you've reached the front desk.

Guest: This is Room 205. My air conditioner isn't working at all. It's so uncomfortable!

Front desk clerk: Oh, **I'm terribly sorry.** I will send someone to check on it right away. Room 205… Is this Mr. Chen?

Guest: That's right.

Front desk clerk: Mr. Chen, **I apologize for the inconvenience.** Please wait just a little while. I am calling the **Engineering Department** right now to deal with the problem.

Guest: OK. I'll be here.

Front desk clerk: **Thank you for your understanding.**

[Scene 2: At a hotel]

Front desk clerk: Good afternoon. This is the front desk. May I help you?

Guest: Well, I certainly hope you can. I just checked in, and came up to my room to find that there is no view! I requested an **ocean view room**!

Front desk clerk: Oh, I see. Is this Mr. Rex from Room 211?

Guest: Yes.

Front desk clerk: I'm very sorry, Mr. Rex, but it seems we don't have any record of your requesting an ocean view room. I suppose there's been some mistake. **It must be very upsetting for you.**

Guest: Yes, it is. I certainly hope you will move me to a room with an ocean view.

Front desk clerk: Well, **I will see what we can do for you**, Mr. Rex… Would you like to come down to the lobby and wait while I sort things out? **We will be happy to** serve you a **complimentary** drink.

Guest: Oh, all right. I'll be right down.

Front desk clerk: Thank you. **I appreciate your understanding.** You can leave your luggage in the room, and our porter will take care of it.

Vocabulary and Useful Expressions

I'm terribly sorry.
「大変申し訳ございません」
お客様の苦情が無茶に聞こえても、とりあえず低姿勢を見せることが相手をなだめる第一歩です。

I/We apologize for the inconvenience.
「ご迷惑をおかけいたしまして申し訳ございません」

Engineering Department
「技術部門」
ホテル内の設備などの修理や管理を行う部門です。Engineering Division ともいいます。

Thank you for your understanding.
「ご理解いただきありがとうございます」
相手が理解のある寛容な人であるというメッセージも必ず付け加えましょう。

ocean view room
「オーシャンビューの（海が見渡せる）部屋」
park view room、city view room、partial（部分的）ocean view room、garden view room などがあり、料金設定が異なります。

It must be very upsetting for you.
「それは大変お困りと思います」
相手に同情を示すことは、相手をなだめるための大切な手法です。

I will see what we can do for you.
「善処させていただきます」
真摯な態度を示すことも大切です。結果的にお客様の要望どおりにならなくとも、精一杯取り組む姿勢を見せることで納得してもらえることが多々あります。

We will be happy to…
「喜んで…いたします」
接客場面でよく使う表現です。

complimentary
「無料の、サービスの」
complimentary breakfast、complimentary beverage、complimentary shuttle bus などがよく使われます。

I appreciate your understanding.
「ご理解いただきありがとうございます」
上記の Thank you for your understanding. よりさらに感謝の念がこもります。

Travel

Airline

Hotel

Column

宿坊での宿泊体験

宿泊にはホテルや旅館などいろいろな選択肢がありますが、訪日客の間で話題になっているのが宿坊での宿泊です。宿坊とは本来は神社やお寺の宮司や僧侶、または参拝者のための宿泊施設でしたが、今は時代のニーズを反映し、一般客も受け入れるようになりました。宿坊では座禅や読経などの修行体験ができることも人気です。高野山や京都などには外国語対応の社寺もあり、訪日客にぜひこの珍しい宿泊体験を勧めてみてはどうでしょうか。

Pair Speaking Practice

A We'll be happy to...を使って、お客様のリクエストに応対しましょう。

Guest: [1]I've arrived here early. Can I wait here?

Front desk clerk: **Sure. We will be happy to** [2]serve you a complimentary drink.

	1	**2**
1st Time	Can you give me a hand with my suitcases?	take them to your room
2nd Time	I need to go to the airport by taxi.	call a taxi for you
3rd Time	I'd like to arrange a birthday dinner for my wife.	help you with that

B 宿泊中のお客様が怒っています。枠内の表現を参考に、おわびの気持ちを伝える練習をしましょう。

> - I'm terribly sorry.
> - I/We apologize for the inconvenience.
> - It must be very upsetting for you.
> - I will see what I can do for you.

Guest: My TV is not working!

Front desk clerk: _____

Guest: And my room has not been cleaned yet!

Front desk clerk: _____

Guest: Also, the people next door are very noisy!

Front desk clerk: _____

Guest: *think of other problems*

Front desk clerk: _____

Role Play お客様の苦情に対処しましょう。
必要なセリフをダイアログから抜き出して覚え、交替でロールプレイをしてみましょう。

Student A	Student B
You are a hotel front desk clerk. Try to answer your guest's complaints.	**[Situation 1]** You are a guest at a hotel. Your air conditioner does not work. It's very hot and uncomfortable. Call the front desk and complain. **[Situation 2]** You are a guest at a hotel. You checked in and found out your room has no view. You can only see the wall of the next building. Call the front desk and demand a room with a park view.

Topic Reading 1 次のインタビュー記事を読んで、正誤問題に答えましょう。

Interviewer: Mr. Hawkins, as a service manager at the world-renowned Foreststar Hotel, I'd like to ask you what your hotel's philosophies about service are.

Mr. Hawkins: Yes. Our hotel staff always keeps in mind three mottoes in mind. First, "We treat our guests the way that we would want to be treated." Second, "Every employee is responsible for keeping our hotel spotlessly clean." Thirdly, "We greet guests with a smile and use appropriate language."

Interviewer: Can you explain more about the first one?

Mr. Hawkins: Well, services can be very situational. We have a basic manual for service, but the manual doesn't work for all cases. In any situation where the manual doesn't really apply, we try to think how "I" want to be treated in this particular situation. I think this motto helps us offer very personalized service to our guests.

Interviewer: How do you deal with difficult customers?

Mr. Hawkins: I used to try to like all the guests, even those difficult guests. To tell you the truth, it was very hard. It is not easy to like someone who is very rude to you. So, I decided that instead of liking every guest, I should try my best to be liked by all the guests. That change in my thinking made it easier to deal with difficult customers. I always do my best to be liked by those customers, and I enjoy that process.

Interviewer: Can you give some advice to students who wish to work at hotels in the future? What kind of personality do you think is necessary for working at hotels?

Mr. Hawkins: Well, I think someone who is flexible and cooperative. You also must be good at dealing with people and have good communication skills.

Vocabulary Notes ▪ philosophy「理念」 ▪ appropriate language「適切な言葉遣い」

Travel / Airline / Hotel

1. There are three service mottos at Foreststar Hotel. ☐ True ☐ False

2. At this hotel, keeping the hotel clean is the responsibility of the cleaning staff only. ☐ True ☐ False

3. Service is always based on the hotel service manual. ☐ True ☐ False

4. Mr. Hawkins tries to like every guest, and this helps him to deal with difficult guests. ☐ True ☐ False

5. Mr. Hawkins thinks it requires flexibility to work at hotels. ☐ True ☐ False

Dealing with Guests' Complaints

Guest complaints are unavoidable if you work at a hotel. It is important to know how to handle them. The most important rule is to take action immediately. If you don't do that, the guests will feel dissatisfied. You don't want any guests leaving your hotel dissatisfied. Make sure to follow the steps described below.

Step 1: Listen to your guest well and find out what the causes of the problem are.

Step 2: Acknowledge the complaint and come up with the best solution.

Step 3: Tell your guest about the solution and its procedure. Make sure to check with them about whether the procedure is acceptable.

Step 4: Try your best to resolve the problem.

Step 5: Report to your superior, if you couldn't solve the problem. Your superior must follow up.

Step 6: Confirm with the guest that the problem is completely resolved.

Vocabulary Notes ▪ superior「上司」 ▪ unavoidable「避けられない」

Q1 What is the most important rule in dealing with guest complaints?

_____

Q2 Which step is the actual action taken to solve the problem?

_____

Q3 If you can't solve the problem, what should you do?

_____

Q4 What do you need to do after the problem is solved?

_____

Traveling Further

Many hotels have the philosophy (or motto, credo, principle, vision, mission, slogan) of keeping a high service standard. Search for hotel websites and find some of these philosophies. Share your findings in class.

Unit 15

Sending guests off

チェックアウトは、朝の一定の時間に集中するのでしばしば長い列ができます。滞在の最後まで良い印象が残るように、列で待つお客様にも気を遣いながら、一人一人のお客様を大切にお礼とお別れをしたいものです。

Warm-up　チェックアウト時の精算の際には、金額を読み上げることが必要になります。

Q1 Read the numbers aloud and write them out.　 36

24,778 yen	
113,400 yen	

Q2 Write down two random prices and read them out to your partner.

Your price	yen	yen
Your partner's price	yen	yen

Listening　チェックアウトする宿泊客 (女性) とホテルスタッフ (男性) のダイアログを聞いてみましょう。 37

A　Listen to the audio and check True or False.

[Scene 1]　**1.** The bellboy accepted a tip. ☐ True ☐ False

[Scene 2]　**2.** The total amount of the bill was 13,600 yen. ☐ True ☐ False

　3. Ms. Shipman will pay by credit card. ☐ True ☐ False

B　Listen again and answer the following questions.

[Scene 1]　**1.** What is the guest's room number?

_____

　2. How many suitcases did the guest want the bellboy to take?

_____

[Scene 2]　**3.** Where does the guest need to go to change her yen to U.S. dollars?

_____

Travel　Airline　Hotel

[Scene 1: Before checking out]

Bell captain:	Bell captain. May I help you?
Guest:	Yes, I need to have my luggage taken down. I am checking out.
Bell captain:	Certainly. One of our bellboys will be up to help you.
Guest:	Thank you. I'm in Room 908.

(In front of the guest's room)

Bellboy:	Hello. I am here for your luggage.
Guest:	Thank you. Take these two suitcases down, please. I will come down in a minute. Oh, here you go. *(Trying to give him 500 yen)*
Bellboy:	Oh, that is very kind of you, but I'm afraid we are not allowed to accept **tips**.

[Scene 2: At the front desk]

Guest:	I'm checking out. Here is my key.
Front desk clerk:	Certainly. Just a moment, please... Ms. Shipman, here is your **bill**. This is your grand total—36,000 yen. **How would you like to make your payment?**
Guest:	I'd like to pay in cash.
Front desk clerk:	Certainly.
Guest:	Here is 40,000 yen. Can I get the change in U.S. dollars?
Front desk clerk:	I'm afraid we don't exchange currency at the front desk. **Would you mind going** to the **foreign exchange** window at the corner over there**?**
Guest:	No problem.
Front desk clerk:	Here is your change and receipt.
Guest:	Thank you.
Front desk clerk:	We hope you enjoyed your stay. Have a safe trip back home, Ms. Shipman.

Vocabulary and Useful Expressions

tip	「チップ」 英語での発音は「ティップ」に近いので注意が必要です。gratuity ともいいます。日本ではチップの習慣がないので、万一チップを差し出されても丁重にお断りするように指導しているホテルがほとんどです。
bill	「請求書」
How would you like to make your payment?	「お支払いはどのようになさいますか」 支払い方法について尋ねる言い方です。
Would you mind -ing?	「申し訳ないですが…してもらえませんか」 mind の後の動詞は -ing 形になります。答える側は、承諾する場合は No problem. や No, not at all. などと否定形で答え、断る場合は Yes, I would/do. となることに気をつけましょう。
foreign exchange	「両替（商）、外貨交換（所）」

Column

チップの相場

チップは主にアメリカでは給与の一部と考えられており、チップがある分、基本給の額が低く設定されています。荷物の運搬には1つの荷物につき1～2ドル、ベッドメーキングに毎晩1～2ドル程度が相場です。荷物を運んでいるときはすぐに小額紙幣やコインを出せるよう、常にポケットに入れておくとよいでしょう。レストランでの飲食では15% 程度のチップが必要です。レストランの代金をクレジットカードで支払う場合には、請求書の tip という欄にチップ額を書き込み、総額をカードで決済することもできます。

Pair Speaking Practice

A 料金を精算するときの会話を練習しましょう。

Front desk clerk: Your total comes to [1]_____. **How would you like to make your payment,** *(your partner's name)*?

Guest: I'd like to pay [2]_____.

	1	2
1st Time	16,800 yen	in cash
2nd Time	23,750 yen	by debit card
3rd Time	118,280 yen	by credit card

B 相手に丁寧に依頼をしてみましょう。

A: **Would you mind _____?**

B: Not at all. / No problem. / Yes, I would, because...

1st Time	waiting here for a moment
2nd Time	giving this voucher to the bell captain
3rd Time	calling housekeeping when you come back
4th Time	*think of your own*

Role Play お客様のチェックアウトに応対しましょう。
必要なセリフをダイアログから抜き出して覚え、交替でロールプレイをしてみましょう。

Student A	Student B
You are a hotel guest. You are checking out. Go to the front desk and return your key. Pay your bill by debit card.	You are a hotel front desk clerk. Your guest is checking out. Show the bill and receive payment.

Billing Statement

Rm #607   In: **12 June 19** Out: **17 June 19**

_____

_____

_____

Total: **121,000 yen**

ホテルの精算書を読んで、正誤問題に答えましょう。

The Best Inn

140 Seventh Ave. North Nashville, TN 33234
614-265-9911

Billing Statement & Receipt

Thank you for selecting The Best Inn. We hope that your experience with us has met your expectations. We look forward to serving you again on future trips.

Guest Name: **Tom Haley**   Room: **218**   Room Type: **Double**   Number of guests: **1**
Rate: **$119.00**   Arrival: **06/20/19**   Time: **5:20 PM**   Departure: **06/23/19**

Date	Description	Charges	Credits
06/20/19	Room	119.00	
06/21/19	Breakfast	25.00	
06/21/19	Valet Parking	20.00	
06/21/19	Room	119.00	
06/22/19	Lounge Bar	12.00	
06/22/19	Room	119.00	
06/23/19	Tax	33.03	
06/23/19	Visa Payment		−447.03
	Balance	0.00	

Retain this receipt for your records.
Reward club member: #8769879   You've earned 45 points during your stay!
Your total points earned since enrollment: 687 points

Vocabulary Notes
- billing statement and receipt「請求書兼領収証〔支払い完了後に支払い済みの印を押し領収証として渡す形式のもの〕」
- charge「料金」 ■ valet parking「係員付きの駐車サービス〔駐車係がキーを預かって車を移動する方式〕」
- enrollment「加入」

Travel
Airline
Hotel

1. Mr. Haley stayed at this hotel for four nights.   ☐ True ☐ False
2. Mr. Haley stayed in a single room.   ☐ True ☐ False
3. Tax is added to the amount.   ☐ True ☐ False
4. Mr. Haley paid by credit card.   ☐ True ☐ False
5. Mr. Haley received 687 points on the reward program during this stay.   ☐ True ☐ False

BRENDAN HOTELS & RESORTS

Express Check-out

Thank you for staying with us. If you would like to take advantage of our Express Check-out service, please review the charges on your bill enclosed in this envelope. Then complete the information below. On your way out, simply leave this card and your room keys with the Front Desk. Your credit card will be charged for the amount shown on this bill.

Name

Room Number

Signature

I have reviewed my charges and they are correct. Please process my account through my credit card.

Check-out time is 12:00 noon.

Q1 What is enclosed with this letter?

_____

Q2 With Express Check-out, how do you pay the charge?

_____

Q3 When you leave your hotel with Express Check-out, what do you need to give to the front desk?

_____

Q4 What do you think are the advantages of Express Check-out? Write down your own answers.

_____

Traveling Further

Decide on one destination you would like to visit. Search for different hotels and choose one hotel to stay at. Why did you choose that particular hotel? What factors affected your decision (for example, convenience, rooms, facilities, rates, safety, atmosphere, etc.)? Share your choice with your classmates.

Appendices

Appendix 1 接客のための基本英語表現集

1 相手に対し許可を得る場合 (…してもよろしいですか)

May I...? / Could I...?

- May I have your name, please?
- Could I see your passport, please?

2 相手に何かをお願いしたい場合 (…してはいただけませんか)

Will you..., please? / Could you..., please?
Would you..., please? / Would you mind -ing?

- Will you sign here, please?
- Could you put your luggage on the scales, please?
- Would you fill out this form, please?
- Would you mind going to the foreign exchange window?

3 相手の意向を聞く場合 (…なさりたいですか)

Would you like to...? / 疑問詞 + would you like to...?

- Would you like to take this tour?
- How would you like to make your payment?

4 相手に何かを勧める場合 (…はいかがでしょうか)

Would you like ___名詞___? / Would you care for ___名詞___?

- Would you like some coffee?
- Would you care for a blanket?

5 相手に自分が何かをする提案をする場合 (…いたしましょうか)

Shall I...? / Would you like me to...?

- Shall I bring some baby food for your baby?
- Would you like me to call a porter for you?

6 挨拶

- Good morning, sir.
- Good afternoon, madam.
- Good evening, sir.
- Good night, madam.〔就寝前〕
- May I help you? / How may I help you? (いらっしゃいませ。ご用件は?)
- Have a nice/good day (stay, trip, flight, time).〔別れ際に状況に応じて使用〕

Phonetic Codes （観光業界で使用頻度の高いアルファベット確認コード）

Letter	Pattern 1	Pattern 2
A	Able	America
B	Baker	Bombay
C	Charlie	China
D	Dog	Denmark
E	Easy	England
F	Fox	France
G	George	Germany
H	How	Hong Kong
I	Item	Italy
J	Jack	Japan
K	King	King/Kobe
L	Love	London
M	Mike	Mexico

Letter	Pattern 1	Pattern 2
N	Nancy	New York
O	Oscar	Oslo/Osaka
P	Peter	Paris/Poland
Q	Queen	Queen
R	Roger	Rome
S	Sugar	Spain/Shanghai
T	Tiger	Tokyo
U	Uncle	Union
V	Victory	Victory/Venice
W	Whiskey	Washington
X	X-ray	X-ray
Y	York	Yokohama
Z	Zebra	Zebra/Zero

Major Airline Codes (two-letter codes)

Code	Airlines
AF	Air France
BA	British Airways
BR	Eva Air
CX	Cathay Pacific Airways
DL	Delta
EK	Emirates Airlines
GA	Garuda Indonesia
JL	Japan Airlines
KE	Korean Air
KL	KLM
LH	Lufthansa
NH	All Nippon Airways
QF	Qantas Airways
QR	Qatar Airways
SQ	Singapore Airlines
TK	Turkish Airlines

Major Airport Codes (three-letter codes)

Code	Airport	City	Country
AKL	Auckland International	Auckland	New Zealand
AMS	Schiphol	Amsterdam	Netherlands
BKK	Suvarnabhumi (Bangkok International)	Bangkok	Thailand
CDG	Charles de Gaulle International	Paris	France
CPH	Copenhagen	Copenhagen	Denmark
CTS	New Chitose	Sapporo	Japan
DOH	Hamad International	Doha	Qatar
DXB	Dubai International Airport	Dubai	UAE
FCO	Rome Leonardo da Vinci Fiumicino	Rome	Italy
FRA	Frankfurt International	Frankfurt	Germany
FUK	Fukuoka	Fukuoka	Japan
HKG	Hong Kong International	Hong Kong	Hong Kong
HND	Tokyo International	Tokyo	Japan
HNL	Honolulu International	Honolulu	USA
ICN	Inchon International	Seoul	South Korea
IST	Istanbul New Airport	Istanbul	Turkey
JFK	John F. Kennedy International	New York	USA
KIX	Kansai International	Osaka	Japan
KUL	Kuala Lumpur International	Kuala Lumpur	Malaysia
LHR	London Heathrow	London	United Kingdom
LAX	Los Angeles International	Los Angeles	USA
NGO	Chubu Centrair International	Nagoya	Japan
NRT	Narita International	Tokyo	Japan
PEK	Beijing Capital International	Beijing	China
SEL	Gimpo International	Seoul	South Korea
SIN	Singapore Changi Airport	Singapore	Singapore
SYD	Sydney (Kingsford Smith) International	Sydney	Australia
YVR	Vancouver International	Vancouver	Canada
ZRH	Zurich International	Zurich	Switzerland

- **IATA (International Air Transport Association)**「国際航空運送協会」
  世界各国の航空会社が加盟し、航空関係の国際ルールを定めています。

- **ETD (estimated time of departure)**「出発予定時刻」

- **ETA (estimated time of arrival)**「到着予定時刻」

- **PNR (passenger name record)**「顧客の予約記録」

- **MCT (minimum connection time)**「必要最小乗継時間」
  各乗り継ぎ地には定められたMCTがあり、これを満たさないと予約は取れません。

- **code share**「コードシェア便」
  1つの航空会社が運行する便に複数の航空会社の便名が使用される場合。
  提携航空会社同士で利益向上を目的としています。

- **peak season**「集客が最も多いシーズン」

- **shoulder season**「ある程度の集客のあるシーズン」

- **inbound trip**「海外からの旅行」

- **outbound trip**「国外旅行」

- **domestic trip**「国内旅行」

- **inclusive tour**「包括旅行」
  宿泊や航空券などがすべてセットになったツアー。

- **emergency exit**「非常口」

- **American breakfast**「アメリカン・ブレックファスト」
  パンに卵やソーセージなどが付いたボリュームのある朝食。

- **continental breakfast**「コンチネンタル・ブレックファスト」
  パン、ハム、フルーツ、ヨーグルトなど火を通さないものを組み合わせた朝食。

- **amenity kit**「アメニティー・キット」
  ホテルの部屋や飛行機の席に備えられた洗面道具などの小物セット。

- **dress code**「服装のルール」
  格調のあるホテルやレストランで求められる正装 (ネクタイとジャケットが必要、運動靴は不可など)。

- **safe(ty)-deposit box**「貴重品ボックス」

- **minimum stay**「必要最低宿泊日数」
  宿泊やフライトを購入する際の条件。

- **overbooking**「オーバーブッキング」
  ホテルの部屋数や飛行機の座席数を予約数が上回ってしまうこと。
  キャンセルを見込んで多めに予約を受けるので、このようなことが起こります。

- **upgrade**「アップグレード」
  ホテルの部屋や飛行機の席をワンランク上げること。
  ホテルや航空会社の判断で行う場合と、顧客が特典のポイントやクーポンを使って行う場合があります。

Appendix 4 インデックス

クラス用音声CD有り（別売）

English for Tourism Professionals
状況別に学ぶツーリズムの実践英語

2019年1月20日　初版発行
2025年1月30日　第 5 刷

著　者　藤田玲子
発行者　松村達生
発行所　センゲージ ラーニング株式会社
　　　　〒102-0073　東京都千代田区九段北1-11-11　第2フナトビル5階
　　　　電話 03-3511-4392　FAX 03-3511-4391
　　　　e-mail: eltjapan@cengage.com
　　　　copyright©2019 センゲージ ラーニング株式会社

販売元　株式会社ネリーズ

装　丁　　　足立友幸（parastyle）
編集協力　　飯尾緑子（parastyle）
イラスト　　ヨシオカユリ、イラストレーターズ モコ
印刷・製本　株式会社興陽館 印刷事業部

ISBN 978-4-86312-356-4